VOLUME 1

golf basics

derek lawrenson

VOLUME 1

golf basics

An illustrated guide to the long game,
getting started and equipment

HAMLYN

First published in Great Britain in 1996
by Hamlyn, an imprint of Reed Consumer Books Ltd
Michelin House, 81 Fulham Road, London SW3 6RB
and Auckland, Melbourne, Singapore and Toronto

ISBN 0 600 58542 5

A CIP catalogue record is available for this book at the British Library.

Produced by Mandarin Offset
Printed and bound in Hong Kong

Special photography: Nick Walker
Book and jacket design: Birgit Eggers
Art Director: Keith Martin
Editor: Conor Kilgallon
Picture research: Jenny Faithful

Acknowledgements:
It would not have been possible to write this book without the expert knowledge of Scott Cranfield, who is rapidly gaining a reputation as one of the
brightest young teaching professionals in the game.
How good is Scott? Well, the publisher of this book, Rab MacWilliam, has
cadged three lessons and is already hitting the ball straight. And if you'd seen
how he was hitting the ball before you'd know what a considerable achievement that is. Rab is looking forward to continued improvement upon studying
this book. In addition to Rab, from Hamlyn, I'd also like to thank Adam Ward,
who remained an irrepressible source of good humour despite the three-
pronged assault of photographic shoots, my words, and watching West Ham
every week.

Photographic acknowledgements:
Jacket: Hamlyn/Nick Walker
Insides: Aldila 27 left; Allsport /Mike Powell 17; Bridgeman Art Library
/Wolverhampton Art Gallery 10; Sarah Fabian Baddiel "Golfiana", The Golf
Gallery, Grays in the Mews B10, Davies Mews, London W1, telephone number
+44 (0)171 408 1239 30, 31, 34 right, 37 top; Golf Monthly /Nick Walker 2 /3
main picture, 45 right, 45 left, 50 /51, 56 /57, 56 centre, 56 top, 57 left, 57
right, 58 /59 inset, 58 left inset, 66 /67, 66, 72 /73, 76 right, 76 left, 77 left, 77
right, 78 left, 78 right, 79 left, 79 right, 93, 101 top, 101 bottom, 102 bottom,
102 top left, 102 top right, 103 right, 103 left, 104 top, 104 bottom, 104 bottom
inset, 105, 106 bottom, 106 /107 bottom, 106 /107 top; Hamlyn 26, 27 right,
/Action Plus 39 bottom, /Nick Walker 2 bottom right, 2 bottom left, 2 bottom
centre right, 2 bottom centre left, 7 bottom, 7 above, 16, 18 top left, 22, 23
above, 41, 42 /3, 47, 52 /3, 60 right, 60 left, 61, 63, 70, 80 /1 top, 81 bottom,
85, 90, 91, 94 left, 95 bottom, 95 top, 108, 109; Hulton Deutsch Collection 8 /9;
Image Bank /Ulf E Wallin 86; Rex Features /Jimmie Wing 62 top; Science Photo
Library 82 /83; Phil Sheldon 9 bottom, 11, 12, 13, 14, 20, 23 bottom, 24, 25, 29
top, 29 bottom, 32, 33, 36, 38, 39 top, 44, 48, 49, 50 left, 51 right, 54, 58 /59
main picture, 62 bottom, 64, 65, 68 /69, 71, 72 right, 75 top, 75 bottom, 82, 86
/87, 88 top, 88 bottom, 92, 96 left, 96 right, 97, 98, 99, /M Harris 15, /Jan
Traylen 19, 68, 72 bottom left, 88 centre; Nick Walker 18 /19, 28, 34 left, 37
bottom, 84; David J. Whyte 21.

Many thanks to the Oxfordshire Golf Club for the use of their facilities and
Robert Walker and Chris for their help during the photographic shoot. Many
thanks also to the following companies for supplying equipment for the photographic shoot: Titleist (golf balls, golf clubs and gloves) and Oscar Jacobson
(clothing).
Scott Cranfield uses Gary Player clubs and wears Reebok shoes.

We're a
to swit
the lig
on.

about

ch

ht

Introduction

There is no mystery as to where the glamour is to be found in golf; on the tee. It might be on the green where a player makes his or her score but there is nothing more impressive than a 300 yard drive. No surprise then that the two most popular players in the game are Greg Norman and John Daly.

On and around the greens might be where the real drama of golf takes place but in aesthetic terms, the sport offers nothing better than watching a sublime exponent of the long game.

The sad thing is that many spectators learn nothing from the exercise. They watch Fred Couples crash a one iron through the blue beyond and they are awed by the trajectory of the ball and the distance it travels.

Yet Couple's languid, almost lazy rhythm and the way he drives through the hitting area is something from which we can all learn. The thing he shares with many of the top long game specialists is that he doesn't appear to be hitting the ball very hard at all. All you macho people out there, who think the idea is to knock the cover off the ball, take note.

Still, it is easy to see how these myths get around. Just walk into a newsagent and study the cover lines of golf magazines. One will be peddling a theory along the lines of 'How to Hit it Hard and Long.' They always do.

What is overlooked is that the fundamental premise about the long game is that a sound technique is everything. Absorb the basic truths that Scot Cranfield demonstrates over the following pages and you'll soon be strolling along your fairway to heaven.

If good technique is one thing that passes many golfers by, another is a basic history of the game they love. This is not surprising given that most books on this aspect of the sport go into great detail, presuming that the beginner wants to spend every waking hour absorbed in their new hobby.

We've assumed a different address position: we've taken out the boring bits and given golf's history a spring clean.

There's also advice on where to play and how to cope with hazards and the varying climactic conditions that you'll encounter.

The one thing I've set out to do with this book and its sister companion which deals with the short game, rules and etiquette, it is to make the sport more appealing to the absolute beginner. Too many give up, bemused and frustrated, when their first few stabs at the sport bring only a sense of help lessness, and maybe even embarrassment.

But golf is a difficult game to master. Trying it without the correct advice and encouragement is like reading with the light off. Trying to hit it hard when you can't hit it at all is a recipe for giving up.

So forget the golf course for a day. Put your feet up and read. We're about to

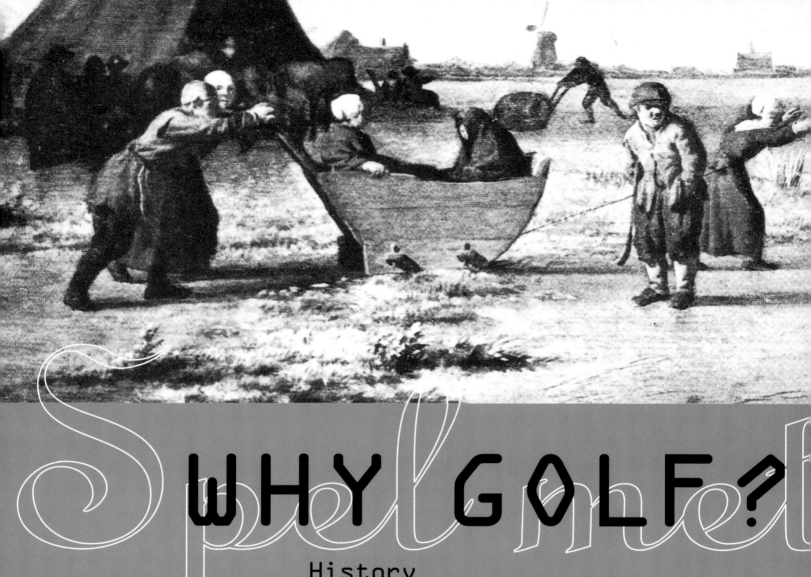

WHY GOLF?

History

Suggest to a Scot that the game of golf was not actually invented in Scotland and you can hear the cry go up, 'What do you mean they didn't invent the game of golf? Isn't St Andrews in Fife the 'Home of Golf'? Isn't the game's ruling body the Royal & Ancient Golf Club of St Andrews?

All very true, Holmes, but the evidence that the Scots invented the game is at the very least inconclusive. The 'auld grey toun' has done very well out of claiming to be the 'Home of Golf' but it may be nothing of the sort – there are several claims to the title.

Exhibit one comes from the early days of the Roman Empire, and a game known as *pagancia* played with a bent stick and a ball made from leather filled with feathers. The early golf balls were also made with feathers stuffed into leather covers. An early version of golf, perhaps?

The case against *pagancia* is that the ball is thought to have been at least four inches wide, which is rather different from the golf ball, although there must be times when we all feel it would help our golf if it was.

With the expansion of the Roman Empire came a whole clutch of similar sports, particularly in France and the Low Countries – *cambuca* and *jeu de mail* were among them.

Enter exhibit two: *cambuca* was played in England during the 14th century where men propelled a ball towards a mark in the ground using a curved club. King Edward III, a killjoy if ever there was one, banned the game in 1363, telling the men to practise archery instead.

Adriaen van de Velde's evocative painting depicts golf being played in Haarlem in 1668 but note the kilt being worn by the man hitting the shot: a Scottish trader perhaps?

ten colve

Jeu de mail, exhibit three, was played in Southern France and here the object was to hit a ball with a wooden club along a course about a half-mile long to a fixed point. The winner was the player who completed the course in the least number of strokes, which is, of course, a concept not unlike the one used in golf. Similarly, the ball was only two inches in diameter.

But exhibit four is the one that represents the greatest threat to Scottish claims, the Dutch game of *spel metten colve* (game played with a club) which was well established by the 13th century and the name evolved from colf to kolf.

The Scots like to point out that this was essentially an indoor game and that the balls were the size of cricket balls. However kolf also took the form of a cross-country game, played in a series of separate holes with implements that were not unlike early golf clubs and with wooden balls two inches in diameter. The ball was even teed up on a small cone of sand, just like the golfing practice at the start of this century.

It is at this point that Scots' historians always play their ace card: show me the evidence that demonstrates that the Dutch used these clubs and hit these balls towards a hole – there is none. Indeed, early Flemish paintings showed participants playing to targets such as church doors.

If we accept the Scots' case, that the art of holing out is the all-important refinement which makes a game golf, then they win the argument that they invented the sport. It's probably fair enough. But whisper it quietly, and for heaven's sake don't let it stop you from teasing your favourite Scotsman.

St Andrews, the home of golf itself, dressed up in all its Open Championship refinery. Golf, or a form of the game, has been played over these links for 500 years.

No wonder they all look so miserable. The man in blue has just told them to forget golf; concentrate on archery.

The golfing revolution

What is not disputed is that golf, or a similar game, has been played for over five hundred years and while the origins of the sport will always be shrouded in mystery, it is a certainty that it was the Scots who gave the game to the world. They were its pioneers.

Golf was certainly being played in Scotland in the early 1400s. We know this because King James II was so concerned that the sport was interfering with archery practice that he banned it in a Scottish Act of Parliament of 1457.

The Scots took little notice. Indeed, golf is often blamed for Scotland's humiliating defeat at the hands of the English at the Battle of Flodden Field in 1513. The Scots' archers, you see, were little match for their counterparts.

Still the game could not be suppressed. Mary Queen of Scots was so hooked that she was back playing just a few days after the murder of her husband, Lord Darnley, in 1567, an action that earned her a rebuke from the Church.

What is extraordinary is that it would be nearly another two hundred years before the sport's followers got their act together and developed an accepted set of rules. The oldest club in the world is generally thought to be the Gentleman Golfers of Leith, later to become, as they are now known, the Honourable Company of Edinburgh Golfers, whose home course in modern times is Muirfield.

The Society of St Andrews Golfers, later to be awarded the title Royal & Ancient by King William IV in 1834, came into being ten years later. These clubs were more places to drink vast quantities of claret and eat than to play golf. A bit like many clubs today, then. It is no coincidence that the trophy for the Open Championship is an 'auld' claret jug.

As the industrial and imperial expansion of the Victorian era brought prosperity for many, so the wealthy English started to visit Scotland for their holidays. There they discovered the game and brought it back with them and, while in Scotland it was played by everyone, south of the border golf evolved as a gentleman's pursuit, and traits of this remain in the exclusivity and snobbery that still surrounds so many clubs today.

Not that you should think that Scotland is free of exclusivity and snobbery. Just try getting a game at Muirfield; there's more chance of me becoming Prime Minister than a woman being accepted as a member of the Royal & Ancient at St Andrews.

Westward Ho! in Devon is England's oldest links, created in 1864 when Old Tom Morris from St Andrews came down to lay out the holes. And so the golfing revolution in Britain was under way. The advent of the guttie ball – made from the hardened sap of the tropical gutta percha tree, which became malleable when boiled – at about a quarter of the price of the old feathery ball, made golf more accessible to everyone. But what really gave impetus to the burgeoning development of the game was the expansion of the railways. Visit the great links courses Britain and nearly all of them have, or did have, a railway line running very close by.

In 1880 there were some 60 clubs in Great Britain. Thirty years on there were 387; now there are some 2,300.

It wasn't just the English who were travelling; the Scots made their way across to America and brought their beloved sport with them. It was largely through their efforts that the game took a hold on the eastern seaboard of America at the turn of the last century.

They didn't just go to that great land either. A number of Scots were engaged in trading links with India and in 1829 established the Royal Calcutta Club, one of the oldest in the world.

A golfer is required to negotiate all sorts of obstacles from the tee at Westward Ho! Some of them even move.

'It was named by drunken Scots after listening to barking dogs. Golf is played by twenty million mature American men whose wives think they are out there having fun.'

US journalist Jim Bishop

The compulsive nature of Ryder Cup competition has attracted millions of new admirers to the sport over the last 11 years.

The golfing revolution (continued)

So word spread. By 1900 there were a number of clubs in both Australia and South Africa. The oldest course in continental Europe is generally accepted to be that of Pau in south-west France, which was founded by British visitors in 1856, but generally the game remained an exclusive preserve of indiginous gentlemen in most European countries. It wasn't until as recently as the 1980s, when Great Britain and Ireland's Ryder Cup team was augmented with the best of the Europeans, that interest spread.

In America, there were no such inhibitions. John Reid, an expatriate Scot from Dunfermline, Fife, is generally considered the 'father of American golf'.

On November 14, 1888, together with a group of friends, he formed the St Andrew's Golf Club, distinguished from its forebear by the use of the apostrophe. Others soon followed, including Shinnecock Hills, which in 1995, hosted the US Open on the occasion of its centenary.

By the start of this century the game had taken a grip on America. It is one that remains to this day.

Recent history

There are a number of explanations as to why the game of golf should expand rapidly in the last 20 years of the 20th century, thus mirroring the explosion in interest during the same period in the previous century.

A prime reason must be the efforts of the top professionals. The game was exceedingly lucky that a group of handsome and charismatic figures should all emerge at the same time – Ballesteros, Faldo, Norman and Langer, put the game on the front pages of newspapers and magazines that do not usually pay attention to the sport, while television brought it into the homes of millions.

Furthermore, the fact that three of them were Europeans helped to make a contest of that previously one-sided event, the Ryder Cup. In 1985, Europe won the match for the first time in 28 years and for the first time on American soil two years later.

The explosion of interest in continental Europe was remarkable. Countries such as France and Germany started to play the game in numbers that could not have even been dreamt of before. Young Swedes put posters of Ballesteros and Norman alongside the traditional skiers on their bedroom walls. Europe had been kissed on the lips for the first time by the sport, enjoyed the experience and wanted more.

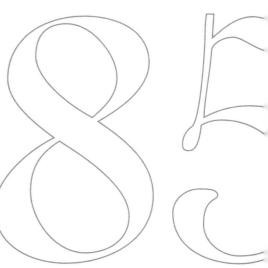

Per-Ulrik Johansson, the first Swede to be a member of a winning European Ryder Cup side.

'Excessive golf dwarfs the intellect. And is this to be wondered at when we consider that the more fatuously vacant the mind is the better for play.'

Sir Walter Simpson

Worldwide game

Asia experienced a similar phenomenon. In Japan there were fewer than 30 clubs in 1945 but there are several hundred now, despite the fact that vast tracts of the country are patently unsuited to playing golf.

The Japanese fascination with the game has reached obsessive levels. It is estimated that nine million people play golf, but such is the shortage of courses and land, that fewer than 15 per cent ever have the chance to play on a course. So they set off for the driving range.

I remember playing at Wentworth a couple of years ago and watching a Japanese golfer drive impressively from each tee, but around the greens he was absolutely hopeless. For a while I couldn't understand how someone could be so good at one facet of the game and so clueless at another until it dawned on me that here was a member of that uniquely Japanese species known as the Driving Range Golfer.

It can cost £300,000 to join a Japanese club and the same amount again as an annual subscription. Many large Japanese companies have bought courses in other countries. The Oxfordshire, from where many of the photographs in this book are taken, is owned by Nitto Kogyo, who also own Turnberry.

But all this does not explain why traditional golf-playing countries such as Britain and America took to the game with renewed vigour. Even when American professional golf was supposed to be on the decline, newcomers were still flocking to the sport.

My own theory is that, at a time when more traditional sports were embroiled in cheating and financial wrangles, the simple virtues of the game were emphasised. The winning of the Ryder Cup at the Belfry came in the same year as the Heysel Stadium disaster in football. What would you rather do on a Saturday afternoon: go and watch a football game and worry whether a fight would break out, or play a round of golf? Thousands of people deserted the former for the safe refuge offered by the latter. In America a similar thing happened as fans of the traditional sports, such as baseball and football, were turned off by players already making millions and who were attempting to squeeze the games dry.

Suddenly the sport became fashionable. Big business enjoyed golf's clean image and poured money into it. In America, building companies quickly realised that a golf course or two were considerable assets in persuading people to move to a particular property development.

The expansion of the game world-wide continues apace: in 1995, Volvo sponsored the first Chinese professional circuit; last year I played in the first Russian Open on the country's first 18-hole golf course on the outskirts of Moscow. On the practice ground, young Russians were practising their swings, just like young players anywhere else. The game has one language and clearly it speaks across all boundaries.

With so little space for golf courses, the Japanese came up with a novel solution – the multi-tiered driving range.

You don't need to know the languages of the Orient, just the etiquette of golf, to know this sign is requesting the watching gallery to be quiet.

QUICK FACT

The volte-face that journalist and television personality Michael Parkinson underwent rather summed up the changing attitudes to the sport. In 1975, as President of the Anti-Golf Society, the great raconteur amusingly wrote in the Sunday Times: 'There are now more golf clubs in the world than Gideon Bibles, more golf balls than missionaries, and if every golfer, male or female, were laid end to end, I for one would leave them there.' Some years later he had to resign. Yes, another convert had joined the flock.

A round of golf on a picturesque course, away
from the madding crowds can be a wonderfully
relaxing, therapeutic experience.

'To really lose weight playing golf the best
place to play is Mexico. Go to any Mexican golf
course, stop at every hole and drink water.
Within a week you'll be down to your desired
weight.'

Buddy Hackett

'Golf is the only game where a man of sixty can compete with the best. That's why golf is such a great game. And no-one has ever licked it.'

American professional Sam Snead

The face says it all: 'Why am I punishing myself like this? Why am I not playing golf like the rest of my countrymen?'

Benefits of golf

A couple of years ago one of those marathon-running bores was given 1,000 words in a newspaper that should have known better than to ridicule the so-called benefits of golf. And I suppose if your idea of fun is to pound up and down the pavements of this land for 20 miles or so each evening then yes, golf must seem sedate and calm in comparison.

The main thrust of his argument was that you'll never lose weight playing golf and you'll never get fit. As if the game was designed for either purpose!

One of the glories of golf is that people can continue to play it long after the marathon runner is hobbling at home on his worn out ankle and knee joints. The sport is a wonderful form of relaxation for the mind and the body as it gently massages both.

It is at this point that the marathon runner hits back, 'Relaxation my foot. I've seen these golfers who get all hot under the collar and turn puce when their ball disappears into a lake. How can that be a form of relaxation?'

Ah, but never forget that a little letting off of steam never did anyone any harm. And anyway, what is the first remedy that any doctor suggests to a stressed-out patient? It is certainly not to go on a 26-mile run is it? Go and play golf, they'll say. And what is better than a game on a sun-kissed morning with the trees in full colour and the flowers in full bloom?

Perhaps the biggest benefit of the game is that it brings together so many like-minded people. Play golf with someone and you invariably find you have more in common than you thought. There cannot be a golfer alive who hasn't enlarged his circle of friends through the game.

For this reason the sport has become a Mecca for businessmen. A round of golf with a client is seen as a valuable tool in attracting custom. Companies spend thousands of pounds on corporate golf days.

And many people incorporate the sport into their holidays. When *Golf Monthly* magazine did a survey on the subject a few years ago, more than a third of its readers replied that they had taken a golf holiday abroad.

No, golf won't get you fit, and neither will you lose any weight, although the benefits of a five or six mile walk, which is what a round of golf entails, should not be ignored. Even so I'd say the number of benefits on each side works out as: marathon-running, two; golf, too many to mention.

WHERE TO

Options

Of course, it was inevitable that, as the numbers who came into the game grew, so did the different ways available for them to enjoy their favourite sport. Now golf can be as expensive or as cheap as you want it to be. You can hit a bucket of balls on a driving range for next to nothing. Or, alternatively, you can join the Oxfordshire where you have to purchase a debenture membership priced at over £26,000.

No game has been more affected by new technology. Golf clubs and balls have been revolutionised, as we shall see in a later chapter. Computer programmes now feature a huge selection of golf games and some of them are fairly realistic, or as realistic as you are going to get playing an outdoor game sitting in your armchair.

Computerised technology has also made it possible to play courses such as Pebble Beach in California without ever having to go there. These simulators portray each hole of the course in turn on a large screen. It tells you the length of the hole and how far the trees and the bunkers are from the tee. You then hit your shot at the screen and a computer 'reads' how far you've hit it and whether you've hit it straight or not. Some of them give very accurate readings as well. Of course it is hard to simulate a bunker shot and the green on which you will putt, which is usually situated in front of the screen, will be nothing like that at Pebble Beach. But on cold winter mornings this is a fun way to keep in touch with the game.

Putting greens and pitch and putt courses are ideal for beginners or golfers who want to sharpen their short game. Most newcomers find they are clueless when it comes to chip shots and putts. Regular games on a decent putting green will prove absolutely invaluable once you start playing in earnest.

PLAY

Left: The driving range is the perfect place to practise your golfing skills and the yardage posts will teach you how far you can hit each club.

Centre: The computer age has brought us the golf simulator, which enables you to play a course like Pebble Beach in California without actually having to leave your home town.

Right: Most beginners have terrible trouble learning a sense of feel with a putter. The best place to learn how hard to hit your putts is on the practice putting green.

Two groups of people inhabit driving ranges: the keen golfer who is desperate to cure a weakness in his game; and the raw beginner who is too scared to take his fledgling golf out on to the course.

Driving ranges can be boring and it is important not to just hit golf balls aimlessly. You'll quickly lose confidence. Take your time and concentrate over each shot. All decent driving ranges have targets at 100 yards, 150 yards etc, so keep swapping and changing clubs and aim for the different targets. Set yourself challenges. Tell yourself you need to get this within ten yards for two putts for the Open – that sort of thing.

Some people, once they have been bitten by the golf bug, install practice nets in their back garden, but here again it is important not to hit balls for the sake of it. Once you feel your concentration wavering, there is very little point in carrying on; take a break.

With the advent of so many new golf courses, one form of the game has really taken off in the last decade: the golf holiday. British Airways even has its own golf brochure now. There's hardly a developed place in the world you can't go and play golf for a week or two. Some places, like Myrtle Beach in South Carolina, have golf courses laid almost end to end. Some of them are terrific too, but then, given that there are some 80 to choose from over a 60 mile stretch, you would rather hope so, wouldn't you?

Another branch of the game that has expanded rapidly is society golf. In fact the first society, Lloyd's of London, is more than 100 years old, but a myriad has sprung into existence in recent times.

But by far the most popular ways to play the game are at municipal golf clubs and by membership of a private club, and these are dealt with overleaf.

'Know what I really feel about St Andrews? I feel like I'm back visiting an old grandmother. She's crotchety and eccentric, but also elegant and anyone who doesn't fall in love with her has no imagination.'

American professional Tony Lema

Municipal golf

The local municipal is the place where the vast majority of people learn to play their golf. Some never leave. Some municipal courses are so good that you don't blame them.

Sadly, a few local authorities milk the municipal courses for all the money they can make, which can be a substantial amount. If you think that a municipal can cater for 100,000 rounds a year at about £6 a round, then clearly if most of that money is poured back into the club, you should have a course and an establishment of which to be proud. Unfortunately some councils spend just a fraction of that sum. At one course in the Britain two summers ago, golfers were playing off mats in the middle of the summer because the tees didn't have a single blade of grass – a scandalous state of affairs at a course with a turnover in excess of £500,000.

Of course there is a great deal of snobbery attached to golf and some people would rather give up the game than go near the local municipal. But the world's most famous golf course, the Old Course at St Andrews, is a municipal and there are many others up and down the country which offer a standard of play that bears favourable comparison with the private clubs in the area.

Municipal courses fell into disrepute during the golf boom at the turn of the decade. The stories were legion of people coming out of the pub on a Saturday night, parking their cars in the municipal car park and sleeping in the car in order to get a game on a Sunday morning. Most clubs have sorted out this nonsense now and operate an advance booking system.

Of course, patience is a word that most municipal golfers learn to have in abundance. Patience when the course is not of the standard they would like; mostly, patience with their fellow human beings, some of whom don't have the first clue with regard to the game's etiquette.

My advice for a complete beginner is to go to a driving range or a field and at least learn the rudiments of the game before progressing to municipal level. You'll make life easier both on yourself and your fellow golfers.

A number of pay-as-you-play courses have sprung up around the country. Like municipals these are open for all golfers to play, the difference being that they are proprietor-owned and are generally in reasonable condition. They're usually more expensive too, although many offer value for money.

Above: The Royal & Ancient is the most famous pay-as-you-play club. This is the New Course, which in fact is anything but, dating back to 1895.

Left: The Belfry, scene of three Ryder Cup matches, is open to all golfers on a pay-as-you-play basis.

'There's no such thing as a bad course. Courses are like people – each has its own personality. You have to challenge each one as it comes along.'

American golfer Barbara Mizrahie

Private clubs

For some people, getting into the local private club far outweighs, say, a measly promotion at work. It is an ambition and it can take years. It involves going before a selection committee and proving your suitability to be a member. If the club is a new one, then you might be lucky and get in straight away. If it is an established club, however, you had better brace yourself for a lengthy wait. Most clubs have membership lists of around 800 people and it really is a case of waiting until someone dies or moves out of the area and resigns his membership before a new member is admitted.

There are some clubs, such as Augusta National in Georgia, where you don't apply to be a member at all. There they only have 300 members and only half that number actively play golf. It is simply a case of knowing a member and then when someone dies you may be invited to take his place. The price of joining Augusta is a well-guarded secret, but as for the annual subscription, the club just calculates its annual costs and then divides that sum by 300 and sends out the invoices.

Each year at the Masters at Augusta there is a party on the Saturday night of the tournament for the British press. It's a chance to meet some of the members, and no doubt you want to know if they are wealthy individuals . . . is Ernie Els a long hitter?

It is no surprise though that people are queuing up to join established golf clubs in Britain, as they represent an outstanding bargain. Most have annual subs of under £500 a year and so even playing once a week it's under £10 a round.

Last year I played a gorgeous course, Bamburgh Castle in Northumberland, where the annual subs were £80. The members must feel like kids in a candy store every time they play.

But, you ask, aren't these private clubs bastions of male chauvinism? Er, are you trying to cause some trouble here? I'm afraid that many are. Some like Muirfield don't have any women members whatsoever; some merely tolerate their presence. At many clubs women are not allowed to play on Saturdays. This is obviously a throwback to the days when women didn't work, while it was one of the few days men could play. Maybe one day the clubs will recognise that not only have we moved into the 20th century, but also the 21st is almost upon us.

Another irritation with private clubs is that they discourage the individual who loves to play different golf courses. The game is in danger of pricing these people out of the market. To play a championship course in the true sense of the word will cost at least £50, with some more than double that. Even an ordinary private course can cost over £30 and if you visit in the winter months, you can find yourself on makeshift tees which are often in front of the ladies' tees. This is the kind of sharp practice that the sport can well do without.

The ninth hole at **The Oxfordshire**, which is one of the most exclusive clubs in Britain.

'Pebble Beach is so exclusive that even the clubhouse is an unlisted number.'

Golf writer Peter Dobereiner

'The course architect Pete Dye's true hallmark is the use of railroad ties, telephone poles or planking to shore up greens, sand traps, and the banks of water hazards. He uses so much wood that one of his courses may be the first ever to burn down.'

Golf writer Barry McDermott

Above: The clubhouse at The Oxfordshire has been acclaimed among the finest in the country.

Left: Augusta, Georgia, plays host to the Masters every year and lunch on the lawns in front of the clubhouse is a highlight of each day.

GOLF CLUBS

History and memorabilia

The man from Sotheby's held the old club in his hands. He ran his fingers over the smooth shaft and stared at its long-nosed face. The club was more than 200 years old. He looked up and smiled and said, 'You're looking at a club here that could fetch a six figure sum.'

How on earth could such a thing be worth such a lot of money? But old golf clubs have become an industry in themselves, with wealthy private collectors such as Jaime Patino, the owner of the Valderrama course where the 1997 Ryder Cup will be played, willing to pay astronomical sums for the game's most expensive memorabilia. In 1992, Patino paid £92,400 for a late-17th century rake iron. Even so, he is unable to get his hands on a lot of the best stuff. The clubhouse walls of the Honourable Company of Edinburgh Golfers at Muirfield, and the Royal & Ancient Golf Club of St Andrews, for example, contain paintings worth millions of pounds.

The earliest golf clubs were often made by family carpentry or wood-turning businesses. By the mid-19th century the leading golfers were often the leading clubmakers as well, men such as Willie Park Snr, the winner of the first Open in 1860, and Old Tom Morris from St Andrews.

The long-nosed woods these men made, and which are of such value today, died out soon after the arrival of the guttie ball. Clubs became shorter and broader and deeper to cope with the fact the ball was harder and heavier. Then came the irons, which did not damage the guttie ball as they had the feathery.

By the time of the First World War all clubs were still made with hickory shafts. But so many were being made that the supply of hickory was becoming scarce. Experiments with steel shafts began as early as the 1890s, but it wasn't until the 1920s that they were being freely used in the United States. In 1929, the R & A legalised them.

The age of mass production had begun and so did the practice of numbering

Jaime Patino, the owner of Valderrama, has built a stunning private collection of golfing memorabilia.

'For me there's something not quite right about using a metal wood. It feels like a form of cheating. I'm a traditionalist and I've held out against using them. But such are the advantages that are being offered that I will probably have to change to keep up.'

Severiano Ballesteros in 1989. He changed.

clubs rather than naming them. Soon the driving cleek, the iron cleek, the lofter, and others became obsolete.

Steel lasted unchallenged until the 1980s. It is still the dominant shaft today, but in grave danger of being overtaken in the near future by graphite.

As graphite challenged steel, so steel was edging out wood as the favourite material for the head. Oddly enough they're still called woods even though few people still play with wooden heads today. A lot of the top players still favour wood, however. It is rather like the argument between CDs and vinyl. Like CDs with their clean sound, it is hard to argue against metal-headed woods, since they propel the ball further. But for some there's nothing to beat the warm sound of the ball coming off the 'meat' of a wooden head.

Metal-headed woods were a liability in the early days with the advantage of greater distance being outweighed by the absence of accuracy. But rapid strides forward were made and by the start of this decade they were being used by virtually everyone.

In the last ten years metals such as titanium, and boron have entered the arena, for making both heads and shafts. Yet more exotica is promised from the boffins in the science laboratory in the future. What price kryptonite by the year 2000?

For me, it is something of a tragedy that the game's ruling body, the Royal & Ancient, has let all this technology come into the game without stepping in more firmly to protect the sport. In baseball, they still play with the same balls and bats as they did 60 years ago and so broken records are valid ones.

But can we really say the same about golf when someone like Greg Norman breaks a course record using clubs that propel the ball 30 yards further than the top players of even 25 years ago? And that's not counting the advantage given to him by improved golf balls.

The enhanced control and power of metal woods has led to nearly all the professionals, including Seve Ballesteros, to make the change from wood.

'Whatever type of golf clubs I use, it makes no difference to me. Hell, I told my caddy Herman I could even win using his clubs. He didn't believe me so the next day I took them out on the practice range and then used them in the tournament the next day. Three rounds later I'd won. It was my fifth win of the year using my fifth set of clubs.'

Lee Trevino

Variety

The advances in technology means that the golfer is faced with an almost bewildering choice of clubs today. It is not only the materials that are constantly changing. In recent years we have seen the introduction of six to nine woods, which do the job traditionally undertaken by mid-irons.

Many older players are thrilled with these new woods since they allow them to sweep the ball out of the rough, rather than cutting through the grass with an iron, thus compensating them for the power they have lost with advancing years.

As for the irons, the heads are either forged or cast. The traditional forged, or blade, iron is mostly favoured by good players, since it offers more feel at impact, and therefore enables them to impart more spin on the ball.

The majority of irons, though, are cast-iron and cavity-backed. They are peripherally weighted, so that the weight is spread around the whole face of the club and not concentrated on the 'sweetspot'. While this means that shots played with a cavity-backed club do not feel as satisfying when they come out of the middle of the club as they do with the blade, equally, they don't feel anywhere near as bad when the shot is mistimed. Mishit with a blade and the ball will go nowhere, leaving you with a stinging sensation in your fingers. But the cast-iron club is much more forgiving, thus favoured by all but single-figure handicap golfers. A beginner shouldn't consider playing with anything else.

Your first set of golf clubs will almost certainly have a textured, vulcanised rubber grip, perfect for use in all types of weather. Many top players are now reverting to a version of the traditional leather grip, again for more feel. It is not something with which average golfers need concern themselves; precise fine-tuning can wait till later.

As for the club shaft, the options are almost limitless. There's not just steel, boron, titanium or a pretty-coloured graphite from which to choose, there's a range of flexes from which to select as well. Not surprisingly, many raw recruits emerge from their first visit to the local professional's shop or high street golfing superstore baffled and confused. There are some useful hints overleaf as guidance when embarking on a journey through this particular labyrinth.

Far left: The grip and the shaft are some of the most important components of the club, and these days both are made from a variety of materials.

Left: The lighter graphite shaft has proved particularly popular with the older golfer.

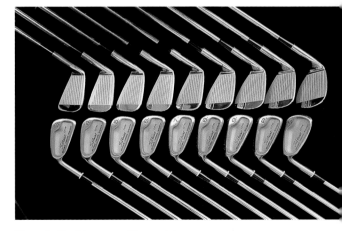

The majority of irons are either cast-iron (top) or cavity-backed (bottom). The latter is the better option for the high handicap golfer since they are more forgiving if a shot has been mishit.

'How are you getting on with your new clubs?' asked the golfer when he walked into the bar and saw his friend. 'Fine,' replied the friend. 'They put 20 yards on my slice.'

Welsh golfer Dai Rees.

One of the best things about golf is that everyone can play, regardless of age. Here, three generations of one family get ready to tee off.

'Do not be tempted to invest in a sample of each golfing invention as soon as it makes its appearance. If you do, you will only complicate and spoil your game – and encumber your locker with much useless rubbish.'

Harry Vardon

Gordon Sherry (right) stands at 6ft 8in and plays with shafts that are considerably longer than standard.

Best buys

Buying a set of golf clubs is rather like buying a car: first you have to decide how much you want to spend. Then you have to remember that there's more than one model which is suitable for you. Of course you can spend a lot of money on a set that may well offer a smoother ride, but if you're a beginner are you really going to appreciate the difference until you become proficient?

My advice would be to start off with a set of game improvement clubs – all the main manufacturers have a range. If your budget is tight you can begin with a half-set. If you're a junior and not sure whether you are really going to like the game, then definitely begin with a half-set.

Forget the graphite, the boron and the rest – a couple of metal-headed woods will be more than adequate to set you on your way.

Alternatively, if you're visiting one of the golfing superstores, don't forget to look at the range of second-hand clubs. Things to avoid are clubs where the grooves in the face have become worn down through so much use. Check the shafts for signs of stress and wear and tear and rust around the hosel. Also check the grips. When you hold the club the grips should live up to their name. Is the grip shiny? If it is then it needs replacing.

Second-hand clubs, though, can represent a good investment if they are not too old, and particularly in the early days when you've still to take fully to the sport.

If you're especially tall or short you should consider clubs that have a shaft that is either longer than standard in the case of the former or shorter for the latter. For anyone over 5ft 4in or under 6ft 2in, a regular shaft will suffice.

Finally, look after your clubs. Take a towel with you out on to the course and clean the face after any shot that has involved taking a divot. Give them a rinse and wipe down after each round or every other round at worst, as the last thing you want is dirt coming between the face of the club and the ball at impact. The game is hard enough without it!

For Ian Woosnam and Nick Price, standard length shafts will suffice. Woosnam looks unhappy because someone has made a comment about his trousers.

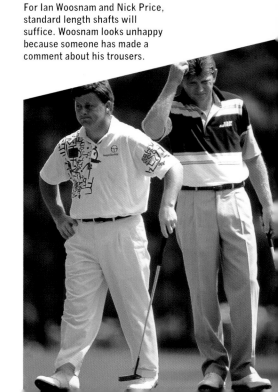

29

GOLF BALLS

'Laddie, throw me that ball.
I thought so ... it isn't round.'

Old pro Arthur Lees after missing a putt in the 1947 Open.

A box of balls made by Spalding in America. Until the 1960s, it was very likely that a third of all balls used during play would need to be discarded before the end of the round.

129   672   108

'Never, never, never will I be able to force
myself to hit a pink golf ball. The line has to
be drawn somewhere.'

Golf writer Peter Dobereiner

History and development

If new technology has made a huge difference to golf clubs, it is as nothing compared to what has happened with golf balls. In 100 years we have gone from balls that couldn't fly more than 100 yards to ones that would fly five times that distance if the Royal & Ancient didn't impose strict controls.

Nevertheless, the improvements are vast even within the R & A's guidelines. Thirty years ago, if you bought a dozen golf balls, two invariably would not be perfectly round, and a couple more would cut after a few blows. Now you can guarantee that you'll get 12 golf balls which conform exactly to the manufacturer's specifications. 'It has made an amazing difference,' says Raymond Floyd. 'I hit my shots further now than I did in my prime and I would say that the improvement in the golf balls is responsible for at least 15 yards of that on every shot.'

The first golf balls were almost certainly made of beech, before being replaced by the feathery ball early in the 17th century. These were arduous things to make and even the most experienced manufacturer could make four in a day. They were accordingly expensive to buy and were easily damaged. Even so, the feathery ball hung around for 200 years before the dramatic arrival of the gutta percha ball in 1848. For the first time, golf balls could be mass produced, bringing the cost down, and this brought the game within the reach of far more people.

In turn, the gutta percha was replaced in 1900 by the rubber-core Haskell ball. With this invention, the game entered the 20th century. Created by winding strands of rubber around a solid core, the ball offered greater distance. It was invented by a wealthy American amateur golfer named Coburn Haskell and such was its impact that Sandy Herd used it to win the Open Championship in 1901.

Competition intensified among the ball manufacturers. Others tried various patterns on the surface of the ball in an effort to make it fly further. Clearly, a ruling was needed to prevent matters getting out of hand and in 1921 the R & A decided on a uniform ball with a diameter of 1.62in. Ten years later, the United States Golf Association, the ruling body in America, increased that size to 1.68in. The two balls remained in the market place for over 60 years. The British size offered more control for the average player and more distance. The American size promoted more feel and was preferred by the better golfers. In 1987, the R & A decreed that the American size would become mandatory.

As the Haskell ball evolved so the patterns were replaced by dimples. Essentially it is the dimples that make the ball fly, as they minimise the effect of drag. Since dimples determine the ball's flight, the manufacturers are always playing around with their configuration.

Two years ago I visited the Wilson factory in Memphis, Tennessee, where they have balls that do everything. They took me to the testing factory where all day a robot thrashes balls that exhibit different properties; balls that don't slice or hook; balls that would practically fly to the moon if you hit them hard enough; balls that don't fly 100 yards even when Wilson's star man, John Daly, strikes them. 'It's a shame we have to abide by the rules, isn't it?' quipped a spokesman. It's certainly as well, because there isn't a golf course in the world that had sufficient protection against some of these wondrous missiles. I've kept a couple, just in case I ever get involved in a grudge match.

Generations of golf balls. The feathery ball was replaced by the gutta percha, but both were eclipsed by the Haskell which remains the basis for the ball used today.

'I don't like golf balls with number four on them. And I don't like scorecards with numbers five, six, and seven either.'

American professional George Archer

Which balls to play

In America last year, I visited a golfing superstore outside Augusta, Georgia, where the US Masters is held each spring. I was absolutely agog at all the different types of golf ball available, and decided to count them for myself. I gave up when I got to 100.

The choice then is mind-boggling, and equally as confusing for the beginner as trying to select a new set of golf clubs, so here's a few ground rules to help you decide.

There are, essentially, four types of golf ball. There is a one-piece ball which is covered in a thermoplastic substance called Surlyn and which you'll often find at driving ranges. It feels soft when you hit it and goes nowhere. It is usually the cheapest in a shop and with good reason. It is to be avoided for all but basic practice sessions.

The two-piece Surlyn ball is the most popular ball on the market. This, oh raw recruit, is the one for you. The skin is thick and is uncuttable unless you take to it with an axe. Because the skin is thick the player is unable to impart much spin on it and so the ball flies further. All the long-distance balls that you will come across are made with a two-piece Surlyn cover.

The three piece balata cover is the one that every newcomer needs to avoid even more than a one-piece Surlyn. Here the skin is slender indeed, and one thinned shot will cut it to ribbons. Even a well-struck shot will invariably leave the ball marked. The thin layer of balata enables the player to impart maximum spin on the ball and is accordingly used by very good amateurs and most leading professionals. You don't hit the ball as far with it, but then again if you hit the ball 300 yards anyway, what does 20 yards matter when you're compensated by the ball stopping on a sixpence instead of rolling on forever? Even a good player damages these balls, and during a tournament a top professional might change his ball as often as every hole.

For a long time manufacturers worked to bridge the large gap between the properties exhibited by the Surlyn and balata balls and there are now a number on the market that have succeeded, ideal for single figure to mid-handicap golfers. Some are made from a three-piece Surlyn cover.

Golf balls are expensive items. As a sleeve of three can cost as much as £10, a beginner should seriously consider buying lake balls, which generally sell at a fraction of the cost of a new ball. As the name implies these are balls that have been reclaimed from a watery grave and are perfectly acceptable while you are getting to grips with the game.

The famous 18th hole at the Belfry features an enormous lake that a player has to negotiate not only with a drive, but also with a second shot as well. A couple of years ago the lake was dredged for golf balls and thousands were recovered. A local charity did exceedingly well from the proceeds.

What do you mean, you're penalising me two shots for taking longer than five minutes to retrieve my ball?

Making golf balls is a precise science these days
and a computer can easily detect a 'rogue' ball
that doesn't conform to specification.

'One tip I'd like to pass on to you is this:
talk to the ball. "This isn't going to hurt a
bit," I tell it under my breath. "Sammy boy
here is just going to send you on a nice little
ride . . . "

American professional Sam Snead

'I was going to buy me one of those Johnny Miller leisure suits but they didn't make them in medium dumpy size.'

Lee Trevino

'I'd give up golf if I didn't have so many sweaters.'

Bob Hope

The red jacket, now traditionally worn by the captain of a club, once warned other users of links land that was not privately owned that golf was being played.

'Let's get this straight: you'll pay me $300,000 a year to dress up in plus fours every time I go on to the golf course? Where do I sign?'

'I wore black for so long because I loved all the Westerns and the cowboys always looked good in black.'

Gary Player

Clothing, shoes and rainwear

Twenty years ago a golfer's wardrobe was so bad that even the moths didn't want a taste. Perhaps the American comic Robin Williams summed it up best, 'Golf is the only game where a white man can dress like a black pimp and get away with it.'

Now just look at what has happened to us all – we've swapped comedians for couturiers. Now the range is not only a place were you go to hit golf balls but also to display the products the fashion designers bring out every season. And everyone, from Marks & Spencer to Armani, are after a slice of the action.

Way back when, golfers used to travel to the links in their work clothes with their clubs tucked under their arms, but as interest in the game grew, so did the demand for clothing tailored to the pastime.

The first golfing fashions were probably the ceremonial red jackets now worn by the captain of a club. They did have a more practical purpose at one stage since they warned other users of links land that was not privately owned that there were golfers about. Through the century the attire has changed considerably and mostly for the better. The baggy plus fours that were standard dress in the early 1900s have given way to trousers made from all sorts of fabrics reflecting the different seasons.

Women have moved away from the full-length crinoline dresses and skirts which required a rubber band around the end of the garment to prevent the wind billowing it just as the ball was struck.

As the sport became fashionable in the 1980s, so it became inevitable that it would in turn attract the fashion experts. Their impact has been marked and some players are paid millions to endorse a company product.

Clothes horses like Nick Faldo and Greg Norman even have their own range of clothes. Payne Stewart, the colourful American golfer, wears plus fours in the colours of teams in America's National Football League. This proved a clever ploy in 1989, when he was in contention to win his first major, the USPGA in Chicago, for on the final day, Stewart wore the colours of the Chicago Bears. Naturally he became the locals favourite and he later credited their support with helping him over the tense, final moments. Some people thought he looked idiotic. Stewart's reply? 'I get paid $300,000 a year to wear these clothes. Now who's the idiot?'

Most clubs have a dress code and denim items or T-shirts are all too often forbidden. Some clubs still insist on members wearing a jacket and tie in order to get a drink in the main lounge, but thankfully this practice is dying out.

A rainsuit and proper golf shoes are not supposed to be fashion items but are essential accessories that you will need. Some players like to play in golf shoes that have rubber soles, but I prefer those with spikes, which give you a better grip when you're playing a shot from a sidehill lie, or a bunker shot where you need a firm footing. It may seem an obvious point, but do make sure they fit properly – there is absolutely nothing worse than reaching the farthest point on a golf course and then discovering that your new golf shoes are crippling you.

Rainsuits are another thing that have improved immeasurably in recent years, with new lightweight fabrics which not only keep out the rain, but are also designed to improve comfort while you swing the club without feeling inhibited. Try on the item that interests you to make sure that you can swing freely, but be warned: rainsuits can be expensive.

Bags, tees and markers

It is not known when and where golf bags were invented. J H Taylor of Westward Ho! claimed they were invented locally by a retired sailor, who made some canvas bags to prevent the grips of the clubs getting wet when it rained.

Whatever, some of the old caddies didn't like the introduction of golf bags and in protest used to carry the bag under one arm and the clubs under the other. Contrast that with the lot of today's caddies, who can have as much as 35lbs slung over their backs, such is the volume of accessories carried on to the course by the top professional.

Many regular golfers have two golf bags. One is designed to be placed on a trolley and will be of sturdy construction with ample pocket space to carry the necessary accessories. The other will be a lightweight bag for those days when the trolley cannot be used owing to wet conditions, or simply when the player fancies carrying his own clubs. Make sure the zips are of good quality and not likely to break or seize up. Ensure as well that there is a full hood that you can snap over the heads of the clubs when it is raining. Most golf bags have plenty of room to carry items other than the clubs.

And what are the necessary accessories? Golf balls, obviously. Tee pegs as well. These are either wooden or plastic and, as the name implies, for use only on the tee. You'll need a couple of ball markers to mark your ball on the green while you clean it before putting. A pitchmark repairer enables you to repair any divots caused by the ball thudding into the green. A couple of towels are always useful: one to keep the grips dry in inclement weather; the other, which you can attach to your bag for ease of access, to clean your ball before putting and before driving off. You'll also need a couple of pencils for filling in the dreaded scorecard. Finally, an essential item when playing the game, particularly in Britain: a golf umbrella.

By the time a golfer has packed all the equipment necessary to play a round of golf, he could find he is lugging 35lbs on to his back.

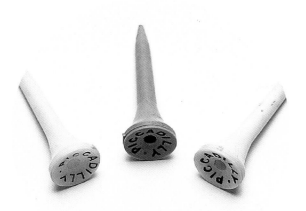

For the first shot on any hole you are allowed to place the ball on a tee.

Golf bags come in varying sizes. When you see someone with a bag this size it means either that he is a professional player or a show-off.

'The purpose of a golf hat? It must have one over-riding characteristic: a large and smooth area where an advertiser's name can be prominently displayed.'

Golf writer Peter Dobereiner

Fred Couples's good looks have meant that he has made millions of dollars from clothing endorsements. But he won't wear a glove.

'George, you look perfect . . . that beautiful knitted shirt, an alpaca sweater, those expensive slacks . . . you've got an alligator bag, the finest matched irons, and the best woods money can buy. It's a damned shame you have to spoil it all by playing golf.'

American professional Lloyd Mangrum to comedian George Burns

A one man clothing industry, Greg Norman's shark-logoed shirts and hats are worn by millions of admirers all over the world.

Trolleys, gloves and headcovers

Among optional items is the golf trolley, which was first used in the United States in the early 1920s. Today, they've largely taken the place of the golf caddy. Most are lightweight and easily collapsible for practical storage.

Golf trolleys have also been greatly helped by new technology. Some are now computerised and by the simple press of a button will propel themselves down a fairway, leaving the player unencumbered with nothing more than a small remote control gadget.

For many golfers, trolleys are an essential item since they take the strain out of carrying a full bag. Equally, many golfers can't stand the sight of them. They don't feel that they're playing proper golf unless the bag is slung over the shoulder.

A glove is another accessory that is an essential item for some and optional for others. Most players use one as it helps to keep a firm grip on the club. Remember, if you're a right-handed golfer you need a left-handed glove, since it is the left hand that grips the club. The glove should fit snugly: not so tight that the leather stitching is strained; not so loose that there's a spare half inch at the end of each finger. Some golfers, like Fred Couples, cannot see any use for them at all. It has probably cost him a million dollars in endorsements.

Headcovers used to be an essential item. When replacing an iron into a bag it would have been easy to hit a wood and damage it if a headcover was not in place. But with the advent of metal-headed woods, this is less the case now. Some players have covers for each iron as well, but don't bother with these unless you're the sort of person who has the patience to replace them after each shot.

As for headgear, a bobble hat is always useful in bad weather. You may get used to a visor or a cap on sunny days as well. Bear in mind, though, that most players use one of these items less for their usefulness and more because they offer a prime advertising spot!

The glove is an optional piece of golfing clothing. Many high handicappers, however, find that it enables them to have a better grip of the club.

the lon

The professionals think the long game is all a bit of an exercise in puffing out the chest and showing off a little. How else would the saying 'Drive for show, putt for dough' have come into being?

In a way they're right, of course. To the American public, the main man is John Daly and they don't flock to watch him in admiration of his subtle touch around the greens.

People love to stand behind a tee and watch the top players drive off. It is this stroke more than any other that emphasises the difference between the average player and the golfer he aspires to become. After all, a holed putt is within our reach. A bunker shot to 2ft we can hope to complete from time to time. A crisp five iron setting up a birdie putt is within the realms of possibility. But a 300 yard drive is something we can only watch and admire, knowing that we can never match it.

For the newcomer to the game, of course, driving is not about showing off at all. It is about showing up without living in fear of making a fool of yourself on the first tee. Never mind 300 yard drives, just let me hit it half that distance.

This book is designed to help you keep your woods out of the trees. If you're a man, part of it is not about technique at all, but about keeping your macho

A good, solid drive is one of the most exhilarating experiences golf can offer.

g game

tendencies in check. Quite what happens to men when they stand on a tee is probably something psychiatrists should study, but in the interim there is some advice that can be passed on.

Clearly the long game is about more than just standing on the tee and giving it your best shot with a driver. We'll take you through the fairway woods and the long irons that are invariably so troublesome to the average golfer.

What do you do when you're in a divot (after you've stopped bemoaning your luck, that is)? How do you cope with a downhill or sloping lie? How do you hit a deliberate hook when your natural shot is a fade? We shall answer all the questions that could conceivably be asked of your long game, and finish off by looking at six varied holes at the prestigious new course the Oxfordshire and how you should play them.

For the newcomer to the sport, then, the long game is not about puffing out the chest, but about conquering fear. The next time you stand at the back of the tee and watch Greg Norman, John Daly or Fred Couples drive off, don't admire the flight of the ball and how far it travels, but study the things from which you can learn: the concentration, the rhythm, and the variety of clubs that a player will use to cope with the differing demands of each hole.

WOODS & IRONS

LONG DISTANCE CHART

		How far you can hit it?	
Woods	Loft	Distance (Ave. professional)	Distance (Ave. amateur)
Driver	10 degrees	275 yards	220 yards
2-wood	12-13 degrees	250 yards	210 yards
3-wood	15 degrees	240 yards	200 yards
4-wood	18 degrees	225 yards	190 yards

1: The perfect address position for the drive. The ball is positioned opposite the left heel.

2: Halfway back and the hips are starting to coil. The left elbow has remained perfectly straight and the right elbow remains tucked to the side.

3: The club is now pointing towards the target. The hips are ready to uncoil.

4: The moment of impact finds the golfer back in the address position.

5: The follow-through; now the body is pointing towards the target with no loss of balance.

One to four woods

Of course, these days they're not woods at all. They're invariably made from metal and they make a ghastly sound when they meet the back of the ball. There are consolations: the ball goes further; the new generation of metal woods is mostly very forgiving and so even a badly mishit shot will travel a fair distance; and they're also much harder to damage.

When you get proficient, however, you may want to try some real woods. Ping still believe in them with a full range. Indeed most manufacturers still make some. For me, there's nothing better than a Persimmon wood. Call me old fashioned if you must.

As with the irons, the number of the wood indicates its potential with regard to how far the ball will travel. The lower the wood number, the less degree of loft on the clubface, the longer the shaft, and so the further you can hit the ball.

The driver or one wood, therefore, is the most powerful club in a golfer's armoury. John Daly regularly propels the ball 350 yards with his driver. An average player will hit it about 220 yards, but many amateurs, however, find it one of the most difficult clubs to use. It is the straight face that causes the problems. A typical driver will possess a loft angle of just 10 degrees. Many are intimidated by it, believing that they will never get the ball airborne, so they try to help the process along, usually with fatal consequences.

Best, then, to start with a two or three wood, which is more helpful. The former is basically a substitute driver and so really only suitable for use off a tee. The latter is a much more versatile club and the 15 degree loft allows a player to use it if the ball is lying well on the fairway.

The four wood is an even more friendly piece of equipment but its 18 degree loft means you start to lose distance. It is ideal, though, for tee shots to narrow fairways, or fairway blows where the lie is none too favourable. You'll even be able to use it in some instances in the rough.

The three wood is the one that you really do need to make friends with. Most players find that they have far greater accuracy with it than the driver and the loss of 15 – 20 yards is, for the most part, inconsequential if you're on the fairway eight times out of ten instead of just two or three. Armed with this sort of philosophy, the Australian Peter Thomson once won the Open at Royal Birkdale without ever taking the driver out of his bag.

QUICK FACT

All sorts of long driving records have been claimed over the years, but the different weather conditions in which they have been achieved makes it all a haphazard business and a bit of harmless nonsense. Perhaps the unluckiest longest drive, however, belonged to Carl Hooper who hooked his drive on the 456 yard third hole at San Antonio Country Club during the 1992 Texas Open. The ball pitched on a cart path. It pitched again on the cart path. In fact it appeared to be drawn to the thing like a magnet and didn't stop rolling until it collided with a fence – a matter of 787 yards from the tee. It took Hooper two full four irons and an eight iron simply to make the green. He took a double bogey and went on to miss the halfway cut by one.

Five to nine woods

Many players become very attached to their three and four woods. The same players detest their three and four irons. Why take a long iron when you can sweep away with a fairway wood, they argue. Make a mess with a fairway iron and it goes about 40 yards, but botch up with a fairway wood and you can generally scuttle the ball most of the length you intended.

The manufacturers, being good listeners, paid heed to this argument. So they brought out a five wood which sits in nicely between a four and five iron. And that went down very well with the average player, who added that club and removed another iron from his bag.

As a player gets older the irons do become harder to use, particularly in the rough. The head of the club becomes entangled with the grass and it takes a certain amount of arm strength to keep the club on its intended flight path (sometimes the rough is so thick, of course, that even Godzilla couldn't keep an iron on its intended flight path).

Given this line of thinking, what followed next was perhaps inevitable: a range of woods to replace all but the short irons. Many older players now only carry an eight iron upwards. Many have more woods in their bag than irons.

First there was the six wood and then manufacturers like Callaway went the whole hog and made a range up to and including an eleven wood. There's something odd about watching a player take out, say, a seven wood for a shot of 140 yards, but if it works who am I to knock it?

And if you're a splendid wood player, but lousy with the medium irons, even allowing for the vagaries in form and confidence and having practised hard, then do pop into your local shop and by all means satisfy your curiosity and try them out.

For newcomers, best tread a more conventional path at first. The laws of the game mean that you can only carry 14 clubs in your bag at any one time. Nine of them should be irons, or ten if you count a putter. That allows you plenty of scope with your woods and certainly a five wood is a very useful tool.

ONE MINUTE TIP

When choosing your woods, do not be afraid to mix 'n match. You might like the 3-wood from one set, but if you don't like the look of the driver, then seek elsewhere. Every large golf shop will offer a healthy selection of individual woods, particularly drivers. It may cost you more, but isn't it worth it for your peace of mind?

Irishman Christy O'Connor was a marvellous practitioner with woods, being able to shape a variety of shots in order to suit different circumstances.

Although this club is still called a wood, it is not actually made from the stuff. Metal has replaced wood as the material of the future.

Most manufacturers make a whole range of metal woods, as a more forgiving alternative to the dreaded long irons.

Long irons

If there are two words that are guaranteed to induce a long face from the average player they must be 'long irons'. I mentioned in the introduction that no shot emphasises more the difference between Joe Professional and Joe Average than the driver, but the contrast in confidence when using the long irons must run it close.

Take the following scenario: a nasty par four with water running in front of the green. The shot you have left calls for a four iron. What do you do? The professional hits a four iron. The amateur frantically racks the brain, trying to think of anything that will avoid using the four iron. Play short with a nine iron even. More likely, go with a wood and hit it 'soft', as they say.

There's no disguising that the one and two irons are the hardest clubs in the bag to use. The loft on a one iron is slightly less than a three wood and a two iron is the equivalent of a four wood, but the margin for error with an iron is much greater than with a wood. They're strictly for low-handicap amateurs or professionals only.

But come down to the three or four irons, with their greater loft, and here we have clubs that are within the bounds of most players. Practice is the name of the game here. You need to spend some time just hitting three and four irons to develop the confidence to use them when you go out on to the golf course.

The five and six irons, meanwhile, should be among the most accurate clubs in your bag.

QUICK FACT

As far as accurate hitting with irons goes, the play of two-handicap Bob Taylor in the 1974 Eastern Counties Foursomes Championship at Hunstanton, England, takes some beating. In practice to the 188 yards 16th hole he holed out in one with a one iron. Come the first round of the competition he repeated the feat, only this time with a six iron since the wind had stopped blowing. When he stepped on to the tee during the second round you can imagine how he was feeling. 'I'll offer you odds of one million to one against doing it again,' his partner jokingly remarked. Taylor took out his six iron — and holed again. Suffice to say that the real odds against that happening were many times more than one million to one — indeed some would say incalculable.

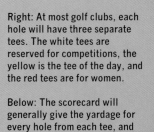

Right: At most golf clubs, each hole will have three separate tees. The white tees are reserved for competitions, the yellow is the tee of the day, and the red tees are for women.

Below: The scorecard will generally give the yardage for every hole from each tee, and provide room for keeping both your score and that of your playing partner.

THE TEE

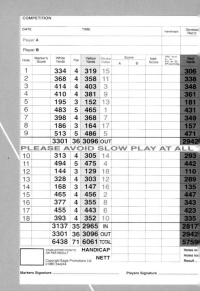

COMPETITION

DATE					TIME				Handicap		Strokes Rec'd

Player **A**

Player **B**

Hole	Marker's Score	White Yards	Par	Yellow Yards	Stroke Index	Score A	Score B	Nett Score	W=H=G Points	Red Yards
1		334	4	319	15					306
2		368	4	358	11					338
3		414	4	403	3					348
4		410	4	381	9					361
5		195	3	152	13					181
6		483	5	465	1					431
7		398	4	368	7					349
8		186	3	164	17					157
9		513	5	486	5					471
		3301	36	3096	OUT					2942

PLEASE AVOID SLOW PLAY AT ALL

10		313	4	305	14					293
11		494	5	475	4					442
12		144	3	129	18					110
13		328	4	303	12					289
14		168	3	147	16					135
15		465	4	456	2					447
16		377	4	355	8					343
17		455	4	443	6					423
18		393	4	352	10					335
		3137	35	2965	IN					2817
		3301	36	3096	OUT					2942
		6438	71	6061	TOTAL					5759

STABLEFORD POINTS OR PAR RESULT   HANDICAP   NETT

Copyright Eagle Promotions Ltd. 01883 344244

Holes w...
Holes lo...
Result ..

Markers Signature ....

Players Signature ....

Different tees

Clearly, some shots that you play on a hole are more important than others. A lay-up shot short of water, for example, allows you a fair margin of error. A four iron over water to a small green allows you little at all.

The tee shot is among the most important. It is by no means going to guarantee success on a hole, but it can confirm failure.

The first thing to appreciate is that their are many different teeing grounds available. Generally a course will offer three different tees: the one that stretches out the hole to its fullest length is usually indicated by a white post or marker and is the medal or championship tee; the middle one is invariably the tee of the day and here the colour is yellow; the red tee is for women.

In recent years this system has become more sophisticated as many courses offer a greater variety of tees. At the Warwickshire, for example, they offer 242 tees spread over the 36 holes and, by prior arrangement, you can play 18 holes stretching anything from 5,800 yards to 7,400 yards.

What is vital is to play a course that suits your abilities. Generally the tee of the day will suit you fine. A course measuring between 5,800 yards to 6,500 yards is ideal. Only golfers with a handicap of 12 or under should be playing anything longer. Don't get caught up in any macho bravado. If you're playing a championship course, don't try to play off the same tees as the professionals. A 7,000 yards course is no fun to anyone over a five handicap. You'll just find yourself having to play a succession of shots with your metal woods.

Left: No-one was ever better at lining up tee shots than Jack Nicklaus, whose accuracy with his driver was one of the key reasons why he won more majors than any other player.

Below: The wild thing himself, John Daly. Do not try to imitate this position at the top of your backswing, unless you want to end up in hospital.

Playing from the tee

Before you play your tee shot take a moment to weigh up the hole's character. Visualise the shot you want to play and what you hope to leave yourself with for your second stroke. If a long drive will leave you with a wedge to the green and you're currently not speaking to your wedge, then take a three wood and leave yourself an eight iron.

Once you've decided on the shot you want to make and the correct line, find something on the hole or the skyline at which to aim and set yourself up accordingly. It may even be the flag itself, but it's crucial to have something upon which to focus.

This will help you deal with any intimidating factors such as deep fairway bunkers or trees on either side. Block out these features and concentrate on the object at which you are aiming.

To help him line-up Jack Nicklaus, one of the great drivers of all time, would look at the ball, then a spot 18 inches in front of it, then the place down the fairway where he hoped his ball would finish, and draw an imaginary line along all three. If he felt the line was at all crooked, he would adjust accordingly. It's got to be worth a try if it was good enough for the greatest golfer of all.

ONE MINUTE TIP

We're all guilty of it. You're playing in a personable fourball match and you're chatting away from the moment you leave the previous green to the moment you tee it up on the next hole. You haven't a thought in your head as you swish away at the ball and it finishes in trouble. There's an easy way to avoid this. Just give yourself a moment as you step on to the tee to work out exactly what you are trying to do. You don't have to be slow about it and take ages, but getting a picture in your mind's eye of what you want to achieve is vital to success. And after you've done it ... why, chat away again to your heart's content.

Left: Nick Faldo is the supreme example of a player who plots his way round a golf course, using his head and leaving nothing to chance.

Centre: Colin Montgomerie has turned straight driving into an art form.

Right: Greg Norman's drive off the 18th in the play-off for the 1990 Open has to be one of the most thoughtless ever played in the event, costing him golf's most prestigious title.

'I can airmail the golf ball all right; the problem is that sometimes I don't put the right address on it.'

Jim Dent having problems hitting the ball in a straight line.

Playing smart & fairway woods

It's a failing of many players that during a round they will just use one club off the 14 or so holes that are par fours or fives. Here's the way they think: a 500 yard hole with two deep bunkers that narrow the fairway to just 20 yards in width at about the distance you hit a one wood? Must call for a driver.

A 320 yard hole with a narrow sliver of fairway at which to aim, owing to water down the left-hand side and trees on the right? Must call for a driver.

It's interesting to note that the straightest drivers of all such as Colin Montgomerie or Nick Faldo wouldn't dream of using the club in either of these instances, unless there were three holes to play and they needed three birdies. Even given that situation, Faldo and Monty would probably still use other clubs.

Many golfers fall back upon the argument that they are just having a fun round and using a three wood on one hole and a three iron on another would go against the grain. Which is fine, of course, but tell me about the really fun rounds that you have enjoyed: were you not playing well? Were you not scoring well? Most golfers would answer in the affirmative to both these questions, but taking a driver on every hole helps them achieve neither. Indeed, driving into the water or into the trees can have just the opposite effect as your score goes haywire and your confidence down the drain.

So think about it – if the fairway's narrow at the driving distance, don't look upon it as an irresistible temptation, but concede a small defeat to the course and use your three wood in the knowledge that you'll have a much better chance of winning a far greater victory by enjoying success on the hole. Or use your four wood if you prefer or if you think the situation calls for it.

QUICK FACT

If ever a shot cried out for more thought off the tee it was Greg Norman's drive to the 18th at Royal Troon in 1990 in the four hole play-off for the Open Championship. Norman had started the play-off with two straight birdies and was in the driving seat. At the 18th, he took on a bunker that was lying 320 yards from the tee to the right of the fairway and lost. He finished in it and never completed the hole. Another major championship blown.

A perfect case for an iron. A short par four, so play to position 'A' using an iron, rather than risk going in one of the bunkers left or right by using a driver trying to reach position 'B'.

Using an iron

Another instance that shows up the difference between the way professional and amateur golfers think is in the use of an iron off the tee. Most pros consider it an essential part of their armoury to have a long iron which they can reliably use off the tee to find the fairway. Most amateurs use one off the tee only when it is required on a short hole.

One problem with long irons is that they require practice and technique, and most amateurs haven't got the time to be proficient in both of these categories.

But here's a little scenario: the first par three you play is 170 yards and you strike a four iron beautifully into the heart of the green. The second par three is 190 yards, downwind, and so you take another four iron and again you strike it well. The next hole is a short par four and the trouble is such it requires

ONE MINUTE TIP

It is terribly important to know how far you hit your long irons. Generally, an experienced player will know simply through using the clubs over a long period of time, but equally, when you're hitting balls at a driving range, take a mental note of how far your shots are travelling in relation to the 150 yard and 175 yard marker posts. There is nothing more frustrating than hitting a gorgeous three iron that is covering the flag to a difficult long par three and seeing it pitch 20 yards over the pin and into trouble at the back of the green.

another 170 yard tee shot. What should you do now? What most amateurs wouldn't do is take a four iron. Even when the logic of taking this iron is staring them in the face they would still prefer to hit a 'soft' fairway wood.

Here the problem is clearly a mental one. You've hit two perfectly acceptable four iron shots to short holes. Why not use the same club when there is a much bigger target to find, namely the invariably broader expanse of the fairway?

Conquering the mental barrier of using an iron in these circumstances and finding one in which you have confidence – be it a two, three, or four iron – is one of the keys to scoring well. There may be nothing like hitting a wood as straight as an arrow, but equally there's nothing more sure to wreck a scorecard than by gambling with a driver and losing.

P

Green

1 2

THE FAIRWAY

Tee

1 Sure you might hit the green using this option but let's be honest: isn't there more chance of hitting the sand or, worse still, the water?

2 The best option is this one, playing short of both the green and the hazards, leaving yourself a simple chip and a good chance of a par and nothing worse than a bogey.

Fairway wood or iron?

So you're in the middle of the fairway, you've got a smashing lie, and the green is 200 yards away. What do you do now?

What you don't do is what eight out of ten amateurs do: dash back to your bag and wrench the cover off the three wood as fast as you can.

All right, I understand. Glory is flashing before your eyes. You can't see your ball in the water hazard on the left. There's no chance at all of your finishing in the bunker on the right. The only shot you can visualise is one that flies straight and true, finishing 20 feet from the hole and your knocking in the resultant putt for a birdie three.

Now, before you take that three wood, answer this question: how many times do you complete that perfect stroke, particularly when inhibiting factors are present and the green is so well protected?

Exactly. You'd be delighted if it happened once in 20 occasions. And think of what happens on the other 19. You either lose your ball in the lake or you're confronted by a nasty sand shot.

I know: you think I'm a killjoy. But here's a far better strategy. Take an iron or a smaller wood, so as to leave yourself a 20 yard shot to the green. That way you take out of play both the hazard and the bunker. OK, you won't get a birdie three. But you will get a four or, at worst, a bogey five, which is certainly better than the score you'd be looking at if you were staring forlornly at your ball in the water.

There are times, though, when a three or four wood is a perfectly good option. If, for example, you're three down with four to play and your opponent is on the putting surface in two, then clearly dire circumstances call for drastic measures.

Maybe the entrance to the green is wide open, or you think you could give Gary Player a game out of the sand. In those circumstances, by all means go ahead and blaze away.

The key is to let the stars clear from your eyes and then assess the shot in a calculating manner. If the penalties for straying off-line around the green are great, then go with an iron. Don't risk leaving yourself a shot you dread. Above all don't throw careless shots away by finishing in a lake.

FACT FILE

At the 1935 Masters, Gene Sarazen needed to play the last four holes in three under par to beat Craig Wood. At the par five 15th, his drive left him 220 yards away from the green, with a lake protecting the front of the putting surface. Sarazen decided to take on the 'death or glory' shot. He struck a four wood as hard as he could. The ball pitched on the front of the green, hopped on and on before finishing in the hole for that rarest of birds, an albatross. Sarazen went on to win the title. His miraculous blow helped publicise the tournament, which was then in just its second year, and became known as the 'shot heard round the world.'

1: For a downhill lie, remember to position the ball further back in your stance as the slope alters your angle of attack.

2: The important thing is to swing smoothly and not to rock back onto your back foot in a misguided effort to get the ball airborne.

3: It is all too easy to lose your balance with this shot, and, because your weight is predominantly on your front foot, 'walk' after the ball.

ONE MINUTE TIP

When playing from a downhill lie to the green, remember to aim some 10 yards to the left of your intended target. A downhill lie distorts the plane of your swing, so even a perfectly-struck shot will fade away to the right.

1: At address, have slightly more weight on the front foot than usual, to compensate for the gradient.

2: Again the key is to swing smoothly and retain your balance. A longer club than usual will help compensate for loss of distance caused by the elevation.

Uphill and downhill lies

In a dream round of golf, every tee shot flies down the middle and every approach is played from a perfect lie on the fairway. So much for fantasy golf; now for reality. Even when you hit the ideal drive, you might find yourself in a difficult lie for your second shot.

An uphill lie shouldn't cause you too many problems. The things to remember are to swing as normally as possible and to take a club higher than is usual, or two more if the gradient is quite severe. This is because the uphill lie will automatically cause the ball to fly up more than usual, with consequent loss of distance. If you are playing into a strong wind, the loss will be quite dramatic. Placing your hands ahead of the club at address will help to compensate.

At address most of your weight will fall naturally on to the back foot and your front knee will buckle, but the most important thing is to be careful not to lose your balance on the backswing.

The downhill lie causes far more errors. This is one of those shots that an amateur perhaps encounters once every other round and the unfamiliarity causes fear. Many people hit behind the ball as worries over the gradient's effect causes them to lose balance and rhythm and to lift their head too soon.

A good tip is to move the ball back an inch in your stance. Because your weight will naturally be on the front foot, it is vital to concentrate on retaining your balance. Swing slower than normal and take a more lofted club to get your usual trajectory on the ball.

Ball below the feet and above the feet

In these two situations, the flight of the ball will be considerably affected. Side-spin will be applied in both cases, causing the ball to hook if it is above your feet and slice if it is below.

Here again it is important to swing normally and to retain your balance and rhythm. Don't try to fight the ball's natural inclination to deviate from the straight and narrow, just make allowances.

When the ball is above your feet, your hands have to be placed further down the grip. If the slope is gentle, then an inch or two will do the trick, but if it is severe then you may have to go down to the very bottom of the grip.

The ball will hook because the awkward set-up position causes your swing to be much flatter than is usual. Lean forward slightly so that your weight is more towards your toes.

When the ball is below your feet all the opposites apply. The swing is more upright and so the ball will slice away to the right. Keep the weight towards your heels to help maintain your rhythm. Grip the club slightly further up the shaft than normal, but not so far that the heel of your left hand is hanging off the end. Flex the knees a little more.

Because the slice of the ball will cause you to lose distance, you may want to take at least one club more in these circumstances. The extra length in the shaft of the longer iron will help you to retain your balance and so avoid the all too alluring temptation to force the shot.

ONE MINUTE TIP

If you're used to playing your golf on parkland courses and are planning a first trip to the great links venues, then it would be wise to practise a few shots from sloping lies before you go. Only Birkdale and Muirfield have flat fair-ways. Some of the others, like Sandwich and Turnberry, leave you with shots of all types that will offer plenty of food for thought!

The rugged terrain of many links courses means that a golfer will invariably be confronted by shots from different lies.

Inset left: When the ball is above your feet it is important to compensate by gripping the club towards the bottom of the grip.

Inset right: Equally, when the ball is below your feet, your hands should be positioned just below the top of the grip.

Divot

Is there really anything more maddening in golf than hitting a drive that splits the fairway in two, you're walking after it, congratulating yourself on your efforts, and then you find it's come to rest in a divot? Do you look up to the heavens and sarcastically offer your thanks? Do you launch into the golfer's lament of misfortune (Harry Vardon way back in the early 1900s made the wry comment that he had never come across a fellow who considered himself lucky on the golf course)?

I suppose finding yourself in a bunker is worse in some respects but at least you've hit a bad shot to end up there in the first place, but come now, pull yourself together. Finishing in a divot is very annoying because of the blatant unfairness of it all, but it's nowhere near as fatal as finishing in a footprint in a bunker. There you're almost certain to drop a shot at least. In a divot, you'll just lose a little control but not so much that you should miss the green.

Although the ball is sitting down more than is usual, don't go digging after it as though you're after buried treasure. Flex the knees a little more and otherwise swing normally. Accept that you are not going to be able to hit the bottom of the ball and so impart spin.

It will run about 20 yards further than normal, so take a club less than is usual. Other than that, no problems. What's all the fuss about?

What's that . . . your ball has finished in a divot and your shot to the green requires a high seven iron over the water to a small target? In that case, look up to the heavens, sarcastically offering your gratitude.

ONE MINUTE TIP

The first time you finish in a divot, your inclination is to leave one of your own so that some other mug can share your misery. This is not only awfully childish, it's also against everything the game is supposed to be about. So let's try it the other way: you remember to replace all your divots; you make sure everyone you play with replaces their divots; and with luck, one day, we will end up with divot-less golf courses.

3

1: Adopt the normal address position for a ball that has ended up in a divot, with a little more knee flex.

2: Swing in an orthodox fashion but remember to drive through the ball in the hitting area.

3: Just remember, after playing your own shot, replace your divot!

Kim Jong-Il, in characteristic mood: 'Ah, another hole in one. That means I have maintained my average of five during this round. And I still have another nine holes to play.'

TROUBLE

John Daly: Not averse to exaggerating the myth of his own outrageous hitting; he tells the gallery he played an eight iron, when it was really a six.

One of golf's great myths is 'keep your head still.' Keep your head still only if you want to break your neck.

SHOOTING

The myths of golf

Like most sports, golf is full of myths. Early last year I followed John Daly around for a tournament to explore his relationship with the crowd. On every hole they would cry out: 'What d'you hit? What d'you hit?' If Daly had gripped it and ripped it with a six iron he'd say an eight. If it was a four iron he'd say a six. The crowd stood agog: Wow . . . a six iron when I'd use a three wood.

At one point Daly noticed that I had spotted his little white lies and found it amusing. He winked. 'Give them what they want, eh?'

Indeed. And haven't we all done this at some point in the tall tale lounge of the clubhouse? A straight 15-foot putt has suddenly become a 25-foot putt with three borrows to read. And you always hit the ball 250 yards in the tall tale lounge.

It is, of course, totally harmless fun. Well it is if you don't forget it all by the time you're back out on the course. Unfortunately, many people don't and if there is one thing that gets more people into more trouble on the course, it is inflating their idea of their own capabilities. You see it time and time again.

Perhaps the biggest myth, though, is the time-honoured advice to keep your head still. You see this in virtually every instruction book. When you swing the club . . . make sure you keep your head still. When you're standing over a 12-foot putt . . . make sure you keep your head still. For the record: it is a physical impossibility to keep your head still while you complete the golf swing. It is undesirable even to try it when you're putting. It increases tension and this is the one thing you don't want while you are on the greens.

QUICK FACT

When it comes to tall tales, the North Korean leader Kim Jong-Il is in a class by himself. In 1994, for example, he revealed that he had had a reasonably successful time of it at Pyongyang Golf Club. He started with an eagle two at the 400 yard first hole, before hitting his stride with five consecutive holes-in-one. He finished with a 34. What a pity he's such a recluse. It would be interesting to watch him beat the likes of Ernie Els and Nick Price by 130 shots or so a tournament.

The mental game

As I have said before, golf is a game played in inches and the most important of all are the three inches that separate your ears. What is going on in that space will determine your fate on the golf course every time. If you're upbeat and your frame of mind is positive, you're more than halfway to a good score.

The importance of the mental game has become much more apparent in recent years. Many top professionals now regard the sports psychologist as an important part of their armoury. The genial Irishman David Feherty is a case in point. He now relies so much on his psychologist Allan Fine that he was even prepared to meet him at 6am one morning on Waterloo Bridge in London because it was the only time that Fine could fit him in!

You don't need to be looking up some Harley Street addresses, however, to feel the benefits from an improved mental approach. Just appreciate how important the mental game is. Here are the key points:

1. Visualise your shot: Before you play each shot you should have a mental picture of how you want the ball to fly and what you want to achieve.

2. Don't dwell on bad shots: How many times have you heard a player say, 'I talked myself into that shot.' It's true, too. Cluttering up your mind with the seven iron shot you put in the water will wreck the next one you play and will end up wrecking your card as well. Forget it. Tell yourself that anyone can hit a shot in the water. Hell, Severiano Ballesteros once lost the Masters by duffing a four iron into the water at the 15th!

Dwell instead on all the seven iron shots that you have struck right out of the middle of the club. If you have a particular shot on your course that causes you problems, or a particular hole, then analyse it when you get home. Is there another strategy you could try? Am I thinking hard enough? Am I doing enough to convince myself while walking up to the tee that I can play the right shot?

Left: Sandy Lyle has sought the help of sports psychologists in recent years in an effort to improve his mental approach.

Below: There were times when Jack Nicklaus was in his prime when he seemed to force the ball into the hole by sheer strength of will.

ONE MINUTE TIP

Undoubtedly the best golfer in the mental stakes was Jack Nicklaus. Is it any coincidence that he was also more successful than anyone else? Even now, just watch the Golden Bear in action and the powers of concentration he employs. 'When Jack was at his best, it was almost scary how well he concentrated,' says Lee Trevino. 'He could talk himself into playing any shot well, no matter how difficult it appeared.'

Right: Bermuda rough is short and spiky and it is very difficult to control the ball when playing out of it.

Below: It is important not to be too greedy when playing from heavy rough. Make sure you relocate the fairway with your recovery shot.

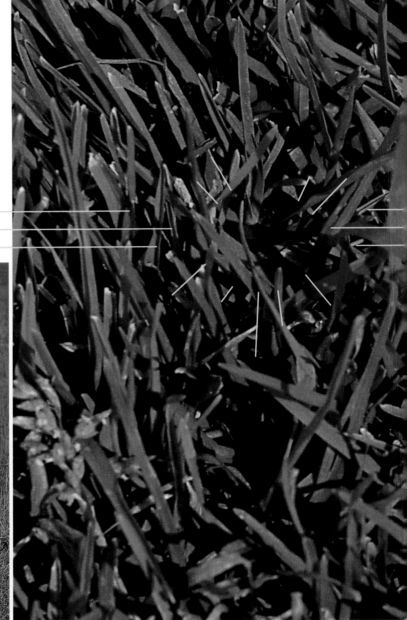

The rough

Throughout this book, the point has been made that golf is a game for all and rarely discriminates in favour of one physical specimen. Playing from the rough, however, is the big exception. Here, if you're as strong as a gorilla with forearms like Popeye, it has to be said that you're at an advantage.

A lot of municipal and pay-as-you-play courses have little rough because they slow down play and, in any case, most high handicappers or newcomers to the sport don't want to be up to their knees in the rough stuff on every other shot.

On a championship course, the rough will come in various shapes and sizes. The first cut of rough, usually known as the semi-rough, lets you off lightly. Indeed, as far as the average golfer is concerned, you can often have better lies in the semi-rough than on the fairway since there will be a cushion of grass under the ball. The top players are less happy because this induces what is known as the 'flying lie', where the grass comes between the blade of the club and the ball, causing it to fly further as there is no chance of imparting spin.

The average player is delighted, of course, with anything that causes the ball to fly further.

A tee shot that strays further off-line deserves to be punished with a second cut of rough and this you will find, usually 15 yards or so off the fairway. Here your fate is in the lap of the gods and your response to it depends entirely on your lie.

If you can hardly see your ball, then clearly you need to use a sand wedge to chop the ball just back on to the fairway. But even if it is visible, do not be too greedy. Look at the grass all around the ball and determine how much this is going to interfere with clubhead speed. If you think it will interfere too much, you need a lofted club. If you've struck lucky, then go with a six or seven iron. Unless you name is Arnold Palmer, Ian Woosnam or Severiano Ballesteros, resist any temptation to try anything fancy. Remember that the object of the exercise is damage limitation, so accept a bogey and leave it at that.

QUICK FACT

One of the greatest shots from the rough was played by Arnold Palmer in the 1961 Open at Royal Birkdale. Palmer had pushed his tee shot on the 16th in the final round into heavy rough. There were gasps from the watching spectators when he called out for a six iron. He nearly swung himself off his feet as he powered the club through the scrub to propel the ball 140 yards on to the green. He got his par and went on to win the title by one stroke.

Trees

Some courses have hardly any rough – Augusta National is a case in point. Woburn in Bedfordshire doesn't have that much either. Both rely on woodland to protect their holes and what a good job it does too.

There's nothing nicer than playing a course like Woburn or Wentworth that has been cut from mature woodland. However, apart from an expanse of water, there is probably nothing more intimidating to the mid-handicap golfer. For six holes they will never miss a fairway. Then he comes to the 7th where the fairway is framed by trees on either side and suddenly the slice that only comes out at such times is there again.

The key to conquering such fear is to focus on a spot in the middle of the fairway and cut the trees from the mind. By all means admire them on your walk around the course, but once you're standing over your ball you should be thinking: 'Trees? What trees?'

However, there will be times when your ball disobeys your every urging and decides to go for a rummage in the woodland. Once again your main task is to exercise damage limitation. What if there's a small gap and if you can thread the ball through it you can advance the ball 120 yards rather than coming out sideways? Realistically, how many times out of ten do you think you can pull it off. Once? Twice? Forget it.

Think about it this way. You still can't make the green, but you will have a 30 yard shot instead of one of 150 yards. Clearly you're more likely to rescue a shot from the former situation, but it's far from certain and nowhere near enough to outweigh the damage if you fail to make it through that gap. Imagine if the ball hits a tree? It could you plunge you further into the woodland and you would be looking at an horrendous score. It is essential to think sensibly and clearly and not get overtaken by dreams of glory.

If the shot requires you to keep the ball under branches, then take a straighter-faced club. You will need to position the ball further back in your stance, and remember to swing slowly and smoothly. It's very easy to swing quickly and hit behind the ball and move it about 18 inches.

One further important note: take great care when playing out of trees. A ball that ricochets off a tree is a dangerous weapon, so make sure there is no-one standing nearby who is in danger of being struck. If there is a danger of the ball flying back and striking you, then for heaven's sake take a safer option. You're not playing for the Open!

Left: Ballesteros is the acknowledged master at playing recovery shots. He can see gaps in the trees that other players do not.

Right: A tree-lined course may fill the senses with joy – but it can lead to a heavy heart.

ONE MINUTE TIP

Learn to treat shots from woodland as you would a bunker shot and don't ground your club. If your ball has come to rest on a bed of needles, than there is every chance that once you ground the club behind the ball it will move and that carries a one stroke penalty. By learning to keep the club an inch or two off the ground, you end all risk of this happening. It will feel strange at first but perfectly natural after a while. A number of players, including Jack Nicklaus, don't ground their clubs for any shot, believing it encourages a better strike of the ball.

1: A fairway bunker shot need not be as terrifying a prospect as first appears. Adopt a normal address position, remembering not to ground your club.

2: Take a full backswing, with the club pointing towards the target at the top.

3: Don't panic on the downswing. Just concentrate on rhythm, if anything swinging slower than normal.

4: The result can be almost the same as if one was playing from the fairway. But twice as satisfying.

The Road Hole at St Andrews has proved the downfall of many a golfer and the crowds always gather here in morbid fascination to see how each player deals with this most unique of hazards.

Hazards -
1. The fairway bunker

It's quite easy to spot the player who feels intimidated from the moment he or she steps into a fairway bunker. Just watch the swing: what had hitherto been smooth and rhythmical is now quick and jerky. They will either strike the sand first and the ball will squirm its way out of the bunker or they will thin the shot, blasting the ball into the bunker's face.

Actually, if the lie is good, this is a fairly straightforward shot. With the one proviso that you can't ground your club, you should play this as you would any other long iron shot. You will lose some distance so what would be a six iron shot off the fairway now becomes a five iron.

Unless you are a good golfer, or feel confident over this shot, it is sensible to take nothing straighter than a five iron.

In any case, it would have to be a fairly shallow-faced bunker or your ball placed well back in the sand trap for you to be able to use even a five iron. Don't fall for the sucker punch of being too greedy and failing to get out of the bunker. If ever there's a feeling that you've just carelessly frittered away a shot, it is when you gamble in a fairway bunker and lose.

2. Playing off a path

In most instances you will not have to play off a path since it is classed as an immovable obstruction and you are therefore allowed to drop your ball off it, without penalty, as long as you are no nearer the hole.

On many older courses, however, paths and roads have been declared an integral part of the course (the local rules on the back of the scorecard will specify if this is the case) and you will have to play the ball as it lies.

Again, this is a fairly straightforward shot, and your approach should not be that much different to playing off the fairway. Aim to take the ball cleanly.

Playing off a path will undoubtedly cause one or two minor scratches to the sole of your club so be warned. Of course you may decide you don't want to risk damage to the bottom of your club and declare the ball unplayable, in which case you can drop off the path or road under penalty of one shot.

QUICK FACT

The most famous instance where roads and paths are an integral part of the course is at St Andrews. At the 17th, perhaps the most famous par four in the world, the hole is named after the small road that runs behind the green, and has been witness to many a catastrophe. In addition, cutting across the 1st and 18th fairways is Granny Clark's Wynd, a public footpath.

3. Water

The first thing to stress with regard to water hazards is how important it is to know the rules. Generally, a water hazard is defined by white stakes and you have to drop your ball behind it if you've finished in one, under penalty of one stroke.

However some water hazards are defined by red stakes and these are lateral, which means that you are allowed to drop at the point at which your ball entered the water.

You can see the fear in some people's eyes when they are confronted by a water hazard. They'll let out an expletive and shout, 'How the hell am I going to get across that!' It is at this point that you know that they are not.

It is important to appreciate that water is there to intimidate and it can often do so against the very best players. In the 1989 Ryder Cup at the Belfry, eight out of the 12 singles matches went to the final hole where one of the players proceeded to find the water in no less than five of the games. In another, between Ballesteros and Azinger, both players found the water!

If there really is no chance of your getting across, then you should play safe and opt for the bail-out route that is usually available. If there is no bail-out route then clearly you are playing a golf course that was designed for a player of a higher standard.

The one glaring mistake that most players make is to swing too quickly. In fact you should be swinging slower than normal, to make absolutely sure that you strike the ball correctly and so clear the hazard. If you're playing over water to a green, then take a club more than you would normally select. Remember: as you contemplate the shot, you should be thinking 'slow', not 'oh no!'

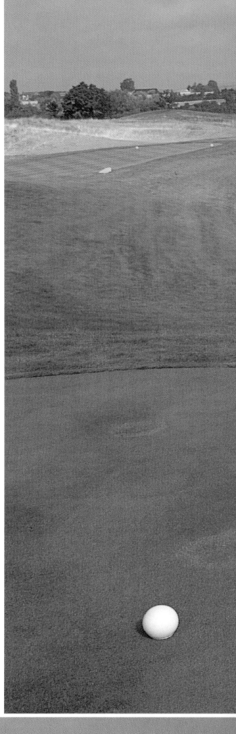

Above: A player must drop out of a stream or burn, with the loss of one shot.

Right: One of the world's most famous water hazards covers the 18th hole at The Belfry, and comes into play both off the drive and the approach shot.

Lateral water hazards offer a variety of options. If your ball rolls into the hazard (A1), you are allowed to drop at the point where it entered the water (A2). If your ball hit the far bank and rolled back into the water (B1) you can drop where it landed (B2). If your ball flew directly into the water from the tee (C1), you have to drop where it entered the water (C2).

'The difference between a sand bunker and water is the difference between a car crash and an aeroplane crash. You have a chance of recovering from a car crash.'

Bobby Jones

'That's typical of golf. I haven't hit a ball out of bounds for 30 years and then I go and do it twice on consecutive holes. Where the hell's my ball manufacturer? They must be doin' somethin' different with these balls I'm playin'.'

Lee Trevino

4. Out of bounds

There aren't many worse feelings in the game than walking up to your ball and discovering that it is has finished a few yards the wrong side of the out of bounds. You feel as though you've just thrown two shots away to the course.

Out of bounds is determined usually by boundary fences or walls, and by white stakes. Again the intimidation factor is at play here. If your normal shot is a little slice and there is a boundary wall on the right and the wind is blowing in that direction, then a feeling of helplessness and a dread certainty of what is about to happen can set in.

Once more the key is to swing slowly and not thrash at the ball. It doesn't matter if your ball goes 20 yards less down the fairway – the key is to always find the fairway.

Remember that your ball is still in bounds, even if you have to stand out of bounds to play it, and that your ball is allowed to be out of bounds for its entire flight, indeed even when it lands and hops, skips, and jumps, as long as when it finishes its journey it is back in bounds.

A perfect example of this came in the regional qualifying round for the Open Championship at Blackwell in 1994, when at the 8th hole Wayne Stephens's drive sailed over the boundary fence. So did his provisional ball. He was now looking at a nine until he spied a lovely white object in the middle of the fairway and upon identification realised that his first ball had pitched on the road outside the boundary fence and bounced back in bounds. Instead of a nine Stephens got a four. He went on to shoot 63, which shaved three strokes off the course record.

Deliberate slice and fade

All right, let's get the jokes over with: what do I want with a deliberate slice when I have one with every shot? My problem is that I'm trying to *get rid* of a deliberate slice.

There will be times when your view of the green or your desired spot on the fairway is blocked out by trees or some other object and that, in order to make the putting surface, you will need to fade the ball, or, in extreme cases, slice it.

In such a case you need to open your stance with the ball positioned an inch or so further back than normal. Instead of an imaginary parallel line in front of your feet pointing towards the target, the line should now point to the left of it. This will make you take the clubhead back on a much steeper angle and the clubface will be slightly open at impact, giving you a fade. Of course if you require a slice then both movements need to be exaggerated. Your stance needs to be very open and you should be able to feel that the clubhead is travelling on a wider arc than your normal swing path.

Clearly this is a shot that isn't going to come off the first time you try it. You're going to have to spend some time on the practice ground and work on the principles, but it is certainly a useful weapon to have. And who knows: once you've learned how to hit a deliberate fade, you'll realise what you were doing wrong to cause that all too familiar slice!

QUICK FACT

Lee Trevino deliberately fades the ball with virtually every shot he hits. The Mexican plays with an open stance and aims for the left side of every fairway knowing that his fade will bring the ball back into the middle. In fact, it is one of the least destructive shots that a golfer can play. When the ball hits the ground it has sidespin and so doesn't travel far. A player whose natural shot is a draw has to live with the fact that he hits it with topspin and so the ball rolls forever . . . and sometimes into trouble.

'I'm not saying my golf game went bad but if I grew tomatoes they would turn up sliced.'

Lee Trevino

1: When trying to play a deliberate slice or fade, the feet are open at address, that is, pointing to the left of the target.

2: This helps promote an out-to-in swing. The ball is positioned a little further back in the stance than normal.

3: At impact, the angle of attack is steeper and the clubface slightly open, promoting the fade shot.

4: Note how the wrists have not rolled as with an orthodox shot and the ball is travelling on a left-to-right trajectory.

1: Here the feet are pointing to the right of the target, with the ball positioned further forward in the stance than normal.

2: The swing is an exaggerated in-to-out movement, the wrists rolling early in the backswing.

3: At impact the face of the clubhead is closed, the wrists rolling earlier than normal.

4: This causes the ball to move from right to left. Note that it will travel further than normal, owing to the spin imparted.

'You can talk to a fade, but a hook won't listen to you.'

Lee Trevino

Deliberate hook and pull

These two shots are a mirror image of those described on the previous pages, but now you need a closed stance and that imaginary parallel line in front of your feet should be pointing to the right of the target. The ball should be slightly further forward in your stance because you want the clubface to be closed at impact.

On the backswing you should be flatter than normal and the club should be inside your usual swing path. Again a little practice is essential here.

This is a shot that is easy to overcook, and do bear in mind that it can lead to disastrous results – whereas a slice will land softly, a ball that has been hooked will hit the ground running. Of course if you are blocked out by trees on the left of the fairway and the green is miles away then a deliberate hook can be spectacularly successful and gain you yardage you hadn't thought possible.

But it is as well to be aware of the pros and cons of the deliberate hook and a lot of very good players whose natural shot is a fade, including Nick Faldo, steer clear of it for the most part because they have difficulty controlling it.

QUICK FACT

Four of the last eight holes at Wentworth – the 11th, 13th, 16th and 17th – are all dog-legs to the left and players who fail to hit their drives down the right are often blocked out for their second shot. Over the years we have seen some spectacular shots where the players have deliberately hooked the ball, in some cases causing it to move in the air by as much as 50 yards. Tune in to the Volvo PGA Championship and, in particular, the World Match Play Championship, both of which take place at Wentworth, to see some more!

1: With a restricted backswing, position the ball opposite your back foot.

2: Cock your wrists early in the backswing, to avoid hitting the tree.

3: Make sure you hit through the ball. Far too many players quit at impact.

Restricted backswing

If ever a shot depended on rhythm it is the one where the backswing is restricted. All too often the player, in an effort to compensate for a loss of power, will try to accelerate quickly through to impact, succeeding only in disturbing the rhythm and hitting behind the ball.

Another common fault is looking up too quickly to see whether a shot has been successfully executed. Any player who looks up too quickly will do so to discover that his efforts have ended in failure.

The thing to concentrate on here is rhythm. Making a good contact with the ball is all-important, so the key is to make sure the restriction to your backswing doesn't interfere. You can do this by ensuring that your tempo is correct.

Restricted follow-through

The first question to ask when the follow-through is restricted is whether you are going to damage either yourself or your club. It could be that your hand is going to collide with a branch or tree after impact, and the shaft of the clubhead as well.

Unless you are playing in a vitally important match, if there is any danger of either of these things happening, it is wise to declare the ball unplayable and take a drop under penalty of one shot.

Such is the force of the swing that if the middle of the shaft collides with the branch of a tree after impact, there is every chance it will snap. This happened to Brett Ogle in the 1994 Hawaiian Open and he almost lost an eye as the shaft's jagged edge came back towards him.

If the follow-through is restricted by a bush, however, or something softer, then the key in this instance is not to let it put you off. Just swing normally. What ends up happening to your follow-through after impact will not affect the ball.

1: This really is a shot that ought to be played only when you're within sight of your best-ever score.

2: Everything is normal through the backswing and up to the hitting area.

3: The danger comes in the follow through, as the shaft can easily break when it hits the tree. Try to swing softly through the ball.

ONE MINUTE TIP

There are many things you can learn from the professionals, but the man to watch in order to learn something about shots involving restricted backswings and follow-throughs is the ultimate troubleshooter – Severiano Ballesteros. Watch how he gets himself comfortable, often flexing his knees a little more than usual. Then watch his rhythm and how he keeps his eye on the ball.

Captain Shepard had no trouble with the weather while playing golf on moon. He hit the ball over 200 yards with hardly any effort; it seems an infant John Daly was taking note.

THE ELEMENTS

Greg Norman's tremendous power off the tee gives him a great advantage in bad weather. Shots struck downwind will sail for miles; a headwind presents no great challenge.

The wind factor

Golf can be plain contradictory at times. The New Course at St Andrews is one of the oldest courses in Britain. If you want to hit the ball left, for instance, you aim right. Similarly, if you want to play your best golf when playing into the wind then don't hit the ball so hard.

Golf in the wind can be an interesting experience for someone who is used to playing in relatively calm conditions. I once had an American friend who came over to stay. At his place, well, if he had 160 yards to go it had to be a six iron.

So I took him to Royal Birkdale and yes, the wind was blowing a storm. The first time he had 160 yards to go we were playing downwind and he hit a wedge over the green. The next time was into the gale. He took a three iron and struck it right out of the 'sweet spot' to finish 20 yards short of the green.

That's what the wind can do. It can mock all our best-laid plans.

Nick Faldo may be the best wind player of his generation – watch the way he copes with it. I've seen him play a knock down five iron to a hole measuring barely 130 yards because that was the club he needed to swing slowly and keep everything under control.

If you're playing a tee shot into the wind, then tee it up a little lower than you would normally, but don't go digging for it because you will do just the thing you most wanted to avoid – sky the ball up into the air.

Everyone loves hitting tee shots downwind, watching the ball sail for miles. In this instance, tee the ball up a little higher, but don't swing any faster. If the wind is very strong then consider a three or even four wood, because clearly the thing you want most of all is the ball to stay in the air.

The wind that most players dread is the one that blows over the shoulder. If it's into your face you can hold steadfast against it, but when it's over your shoulder, it can affect your balance. It's a good idea here to widen your stance by a couple of inches, but again: a slow swing. This cannot be stressed enough.

QUICK FACT

Wind was not a problem for Captain Alan Shepard of Apollo 14 when he tried to play golf on the moon's surface in 1971. With a one-handed swing and an iron head attached to a makeshift shaft, he reckoned he struck a ball 200 yards, owing to the moon's reduced gravity. Mind you, I doubt that the apparel he was wearing that day will catch on in golf circles. The R & A, meanwhile, sent him the following telegram: 'Warmest congratulations to you and your colleagues on your great achievement and safe return. Please refer to Rules of Golf section on etiquette, paragraph 6, quote, before leaving a bunker a player should carefully fill up all holes made by him therein, unquote.'

Playing into the sun and rain

Initially, these would appear to be two extremes: the pleasure of playing golf on a sun-kissed day, and on the other hand the utter misery of trudging round 18 holes getting soaked to the skin. In reality, it is not all plain sailing on one hand, and the other doesn't have to be a completely miserable experience.

Playing into the sun inevitably invites you to lift your head too early to try to spot where the damn ball has gone. Of course all that happens is you end up squinting into a yellow blur. What makes it worse is that if you've lifted your head too soon you won't even have the satisfaction of a good shot to comfort you.

The best way to combat this is to ask one of your playing partners if he will kindly do the honours. If you're playing on your own . . . the best advice is to concentrate on making sure you hit a good shot and, well, it won't matter if you haven't seen it then because it will have gone down the middle won't it?

Playing with a cap or a visor can obviously help to cut down the glaring rays of the sun, although many people find them more of a distraction than a help if they're not used to them.

Playing with a cap is more than useful if it's bucketing down. So is a good rain suit. And waterproof shoes.

Ensure you have three or four small towels with you to enable you to keep your grips as dry as you can. Once these become wet, you've really no chance of playing well no matter how nicely you're swinging, so pay extra care to this. An idea is to hang one under your umbrella so it is easily accessible to dry both your hands and clubs.

This is another instance when swinging slowly and smoothly can bring great dividends. Concentrating harder can also help to combat the depressing effects of the weather.

You could squint into the sun here, like Monty. Or you could wear a visor or cap.

ONE MINUTE TIP

There can often be as much as two clubs difference between hitting shots on a sunny day and one filled with rain. In the sun, the ball will travel further through the warm air and, if there has been a succession of nice days, will of course roll further on the baked earth once it lands. In the wet, the ball won't be going anywhere once it squelches down, so take a club more than you would normally use.

A good rainsuit can compensate for much of the discomfort of playing in the rain.

Right: Golf rarely gets more idyllic than when played on an island course amidst swaying palms and beside an azure-blue sea.

Below: The wonders of modern transport have brought the world's top courses within range.

Playing abroad

The golf boom in the 1980s led to a golden age in the construction of courses and a huge increase in the number of golfers who were prepared to travel to play on them. The golfing holiday is something that more than half of Britain's golfers have now enjoyed and the vast majority of them have done so abroad.

Initially it was Spain and Portugal that were the destinations favoured by most. But the golfing holiday has become more varied as it has become more popular and now the world is at your feet.

Those two Mediterranean countries still remain high on the list for European golfers, but America is a close third now. Places like Florida and South Carolina, in particular, have become shrines to the Royal & Ancient game.

An important point to remember about playing golf in Spain and Portugal or indeed anywhere in Europe is that the hole measurements will be in metres, which means you'll have to add on an extra ten per cent if you want to convert the distance into yards; if you're playing golf in the mountains of Switzerland or Austria, however, don't bother, because the thin mountain air means you'll hit the ball ten per cent further anyway.

The growth in the golf holiday industry has sadly brought about a corresponding increase in green fees. Many people stayed away from Spain and Portugal at the start of the 1990s for this very reason, working out that they could play in America for much the same price.

It can be expensive, then, if you just turn up abroad at a course. In the States, you'll be very lucky if you get any change out of £80 for a round and the use of the compulsory cart at any renowned golf course. So make sure to read the fine print of your golf holiday brochure to see if green fees are included in the price.

What the American courses do offer are standards of maintenance which are much higher than those on the average course in Britain (so they should be, you might argue, at those prices). The greens will be cut every day and the

holes changed. The fairways will be pristine and the whole course will be kept in an immaculate condition.

This has led to the charge in some quarters that it is all a little manufactured and there's nothing to beat the glorious uncertainty of a British links course, with its bad lies, bad bounces and all. And yes it's true, it is all a little manufactured. But equally it's a glorious holiday experience with a warm sun on your back.

You're bound to come across things you'll never see at home as well. I've played a par three in Florida where a couple of alligators were sunning themselves at the side of the green next to the lake. I was terrified to putt because it meant turning my back on them.

I've played courses in the desert of Arizona where putts played away from the mountains in the background move faster than putts played towards them. In Kenya I played a course just outside Nairobi where the green fee was minimal and the flora and fauna was as spectacular as that to be found at Augusta.

In America, you'll invariably find the majority of the greens are surrounded by a collar of rough which is almost impossible to adapt to in the few golfing days available to you. What you should appreciate is that the yardage to each hole is written on every fairway sprinkler head on most courses. If you know how far you can hit each club this is a wonderful aid.

One thing that may upset you is having to play golf riding round in a cart. It's no use protesting that you'd rather walk, thanks all the same. The money gained from making everyone ride in a cart is a vital source of revenue for most courses in America and an increasing number in Europe. I think they're awful and the rule a terrible imposition. It was the American author Mark Twain who ruminated that golf was a good walk spoiled. Modern Americans must wonder what he was talking about: walk? What's golf got to do with walking?

QUICK FACT

The first time I played golf in America I was wandering around a supermarket buying some goodies and the observant cashier noticed the strange accent. 'Britain eh?' she said and thought for a moment. 'And how far away exactly is that?' After I told her she said: 'Four thousand miles? You mean you drove four thousand miles to play golf here?'

Many beginners wouldn't think of practising their bunker shots. No wonder they have such difficulty extracting their ball from the sand.

The driving range offers the perfect environment to practise all your long game shots.

Many professionals now have indoor facilities where your swing can be videotaped and analysed.

PRACTICE

Where to practise

For some golfers, of course, this chapter is completely and utterly irrelevant. Many never see a practice ground from one year to the next and their idea of a driving range is a selection of cars.

Practice doesn't have to be unspeakably boring. It doesn't have to rank alongside doing the washing up or mowing the lawn. It can be useful and interesting. Honestly.

The key is to practise with a purpose. Don't go without an idea in your head and then hit balls aimlessly. Whilst in the car on the way to wherever you're going to practise, make a mental list of the three things which you would most like to improve and work on those diligently. Limit yourself to two hours' maximum.

The place where most people practise is the local driving range and these have improved greatly as the demand has risen in recent years. Ten years ago a typical range was run down with poor teeing mats and even poorer golf balls.

You should now be able to find one locally that is swish and modern. The best have miniature greens with flags indicating 50 yards, 75 yards, 100 yards etc. Rather than just being flat and boring they've been landscaped. A small fee will get you a bucket of balls; they can do your golf a power of good and represent excellent value.

Most of the traditional clubs have very limited practice facilities. Some of the more recently-built establishments will have a practice bunker from which you can play as well as a practice green to which you can chip. Often you can use these for a small sum, even if you are not a member.

Some of you will become sufficiently hooked on the game to install a private net at home into which you can smash golf balls to your heart's content. This, to me, has always seemed unspeakably boring.

Another way of practising your long irons and woods at home is with a practice golf ball which is made of plastic and full of holes, making it fairly difficult to damage anyone or anything.

Patio owners can check a few things by looking at the reflection in the glass. By facing the glass, you can check that the ball is positioned just inside your heel. By completing your backswing you can make sure you are not taking the club back beyond the horizontal.

Now stand side on to the glass and check your address position. Are you standing 'tall' to the ball, but with your knees flexed and your body relaxed? Are your hands far enough away from your body? Now swing the club back: Is the shaft pointing down an imaginary straight line to the target? When you swing through, check that your finishing position leaves you face on to the glass.

There. Not so boring after all was it?

QUICK FACT

One man with an insatiable appetite for practice is Lee Trevino. If he's not playing in a tournament, he'll be down at his local range at 8.30 a.m. He'll hit balls without a break until lunch time when he'll have something to eat on his golf cart. Then he'll take a siesta on his golf cart. He'll start hitting balls again at 2.30 p.m. and he'll continue until they order him off the range at dusk. Trevino reckons he has hit golf balls virtually every day of his life from the age of 25.

Essential practice drills

There's no getting round the fact that bringing your long game up to a proficient level is going to require a fair amount of work. Here are six practice drills to help you get the most out of your woods and long irons:

1. Tee the ball up with your long irons

Now I know you're not allowed to do this when playing on the course, but the thing that intimidates most players about the long irons is their lack of loft. They attempt to compensate by trying to scoop the ball into the air.

By putting the ball on a tee you're providing some loft and so now you can concentrate on the smooth and rhythmical tempo that is so vital to good iron shots. Watch the great long iron players like Nick Faldo and Ernie Els. How often, as they strike another one iron down the fairway, have you said to yourself it's like shelling peas? The secret is they don't swing any faster with a one iron than they would with an eight iron.

When you've mastered playing the shot off a tee you can progress to playing them off the grass or a tee mat.

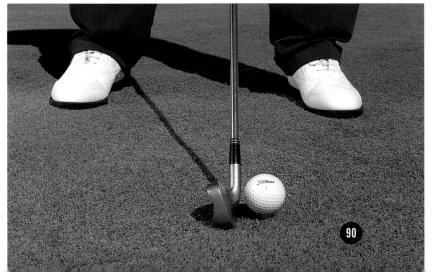

Long irons are the most difficult clubs in the bag to use, so practise them by teeing the ball up at first.

2. Sweeping to success

Sam Snead, one of the great drivers of all time, said that the thing he concentrated on when hitting his tee shots was the feeling that he was sweeping the ball off the tee.

This remains one of the great tips. Just try it. Get that picture in your mind of a sweeping action through the ball. This will encourage you to swing freely in the hitting area.

Practise your alignment by placing a club against your toes, running parallel to the direction in which you are playing. Now step away and look down towards the target. The club should be pointing towards it if your alignment is correct.

3. Check your alignment

This is best done with the help of a friend or practice partner. Line up to the target. Now ask your colleague to place a club so that it is lined up against your toes. It should be pointing directly at the target if you're aligned properly. It isn't? You're hardly alone.

Many players are absolutely astonished at how far out their alignment is when they do this simple exercise. If you're one of those it can feel really strange when you set-up correctly, pointing towards the target, but persevere. Retrain your muscles so that they're focused properly, and practise a few shots leaving that club on the ground in front of your toes.

Having something to aim at is always a good idea when practising, although backdrops are rarely as spectacular as this!

Essential practice drills (continued)

4. Always have something to aim at

A driving range is good in this case because there are targets at which you can aim. But if you are in an open field or on the club's practice ground, find a spot in the great blue yonder upon which you can focus. Better still, pace out 200 yards and stick an umbrella or something in the ground. Hitting balls without a target makes it hard to concentrate and you can easily lapse into the sort of faults that you came to the practice ground to eradicate.

5. Left shoulder visible

One of the most common faults among golfers is the failure to coil properly during the backswing, thus losing a great deal of power and distance. Here's an easy way to check that you are turning your upper body on the backswing. When you get to the top, the point of your left shoulder should be over the ball. If it is, then your upper body is coiled nicely and you are in the correct position to gain distance and power through the ball.

6. Struggling with your rhythm and tempo?

You see it all the time. A nicely controlled backswing. An ungainly lash at the ball. Or an ungainly backswing, followed by an ungainly lash at the ball. With good tempo and rhythm a golfer can compensate for many other faults.

One way of improving this side of your game is to practise with a half swing, that is, take the club back to the 9 o'clock position and then on through to the 3 o'clock position. This discipline promotes smoothness of rhythm so give in to it. After a few minutes try swinging the club back to your normal position using the same key thoughts.

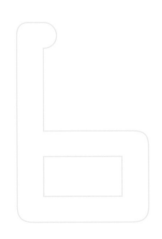

At the top of the backswing the point of your left shoulder should be directly over the ball.

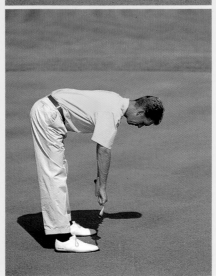

Since the golf swing comprises a series of unnatural body movements, it is an excellent idea to do a few stretching exercises before going out to play. Try holding a club in front of you and bend from the waist, as far as you can, without straining.

GOOD WARM-UP EXERCISES

Playing golf by itself may not get you fit, but it can certainly leave you armchair-bound. A round of golf lasts a few hours and in that time the back, the knees and the feet all get a hammering every time you play.

The back in particular, of course, takes most of the strain. The number of golfers who suffer from ailments in the lumbar area are legion. Even the best golfers are not immune; indeed they are some of the worst sufferers. Seve Ballesteros, Ian Woosnam, Bernhard Langer, Payne Stewart and Fred Couples are just some of those who suffer from chronic back conditions.

If you're hitting golf balls all day every day then it is inevitable that such repetition is going to take its toll on muscles and ligaments. Fortunately, none of us have to subject ourselves to such a regimen.

There are some things you can do to avoid back problems. For instance, when you go to the boot of the car to take out your clubs, the temptation is to yank them out, not thinking of the strain you are putting on the lower back. Thousands of golfers have done this only to find a muscle give way before they have even struck a ball, spoiling their afternoon's pleasure. The irony is that if you were lifting a 30lb weight out of the boot, you would take great care – a golf bag is the same weight and so, of course, demands the same amount of attention.

Hold the club above your head
and stretch upwards, slowly.

Similarly, don't just step on to the first tee and lash at the ball while all your muscles are still cold. That's a real recipe for disaster. Here we've come up with five of the best exercises to help you protect those parts of the body that the golf swing puts under the most strain. They are best completed at home before your round of golf. Try doing them daily if you can. They will take no more than 15 minutes at most and will leave you healthier and fitter to play your favourite sport.
R1 Sit-ups.   R2 Lie on back; pull knees to chest.   R3 Cobra position for bad back.
R4 Lie flat on the back and stretch.   R5 Shoulder exercises.

This is not only a good stretching exercise for your
sides, but will teach you how to both coil and
uncoil your body.

Many courses now have marks in the middle of the fairway, indicating how far a player has to go to the green.

The caddies generally prefer to do their own yardages and yardage wheels will provide an exact measurement.

DISTANCE

Using yardage charts and sprinklers

Many old professionals consider that some of the art of the game has been taken away in recent years with the development of artificial aids to determine how far a player has to the green.

Certainly a little of the skill has been taken out. If you're standing right in the middle of the fairway with the wind blowing a little, debating which club to take, and all you've got to go on is your mind's eye, then clearly distance judgement is more difficult than if you possess a yardage chart which tells you exactly how far you need to hit the shot.

Yardage charts are an invaluable aid to any player who knows exactly how far they hit every club. It enables them to plot their way round the golf course; how to avoid hitting into a ditch or bunker off the tee; what club to take to find the middle of the green. There really is no excuse for under or overclubbing.

Or is there? There are a number of ways in which a golf architect can make a mockery of a yardage chart and we shall deal with them overleaf.

Most courses now have some sort of yardage indicators on the course. It may be a stake or a small bush at the 150 yard mark. Some courses in this country, and nearly every course in America, will also have the yardage printed on a selected number of fairway sprinkler heads.

These are a wonderful aid, but before you go out, do make sure you establish whether they are measured to the front or the centre of the green. On a course

ONE MINUTE TIP

Nearly every golf club now has yardage charts, but they all vary enormously. Many players make the mistake of turning immediately to hole one and wonder why their opening iron shot landed on the front of the green, when the book said they had 150 yards to go and they would normally hit a seven iron that distance. Some yardage charts have measurements to the front of the green; you need to take more than a cursory glance at the first page. So take care to swot up on this information before you start your round, and not when you're cursing a 50 feet putt stretching the length of the green.

JUDGEMENT

where they have large putting surfaces it can make a huge difference; you may find yourself on the fringe of the green with a very long shot to the pin.

Of course in the professional world they take yardages very seriously. Many caddies will go out 48 hours before the start of a tournament armed with a measuring wheel and, knowing roughly where their man will hit the ball, they mark off points so they know exactly how far the player will have to the flag.

This may seem to be taking things to the extreme when, on the courses the pros play, the yardages are on virtually every other sprinkler head. But think of it this way: they know how far they hit each club almost to the yard; a yard each way can make the difference between a holed putt or a miss; one stroke can mean a great deal of money. In this light, it no longer seems so extreme.

Colin Montgomerie tells a very amusing story on this subject which he insists is true. It happened in the 1991 Ryder Cup at Kiawah Island when he was partnering that well-known perfectionist, Bernhard Langer, in the foursomes.

It was Monty's turn to drive off on one hole and he duly found the middle of the fairway. As they assessed the second shot that Langer had left, the German called out to Montgomerie, who was standing a few yards away. 'What yardage have you got from that sprinkler head?' Langer asked. Monty looked and consulted his yardage book. '170,' he said. Langer replied, with a touch of impatience: 'Yes, but is that from the front of the sprinkler head or the back?'

Sprinkler heads will often provide yardages as well. Always check first, however, whether the yardage is to the front or the middle of the green.

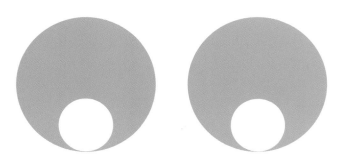

No player was ever better at judging distance than Lee Trevino, who knew exactly how far he could hit each shot.

This par three at Woburn, with the tee situated well above the green, is a prime example of a hole which plays much less than the yardage stated.

QUICK FACT

A firm contender for the greatest round of golf played in inclement conditions was Greg Norman's second round in the 1986 Open at Turnberry. Most players were thrilled if they came in with a score within touching distance of the stringent par of 70. Norman shot 63, and went on to win the event by five shots. No less a luminary than Tom Watson called it 'the finest round of golf in an event in which I have been a competitor.'

Using your eyes

As I said, there are a number of ways in which the golf architect can render a yardage chart worthless, and any decent course will have a couple of holes that duly do this. The trick is to be able to spot them on the tee.

One is the par three with an elevated tee far above the green. The hole measures 160 yards. Do you take the club with which you normally propel the ball 160 yards? If you did you would almost certainly be hacking out of the rubbish behind the green for your second.

Elevated tees foreshorten any hole, and the higher up you are in relation to the green, the less club you need to take. If the elevation is 30 or 40 feet then you will need two or even three clubs less than you would normally hit.

After that salutary experience you move on to a long par four, slightly uphill this time. You've got 140 yards to go. Now you need one club more than usual and again, if the gradient is steep then you may need two or three clubs more.

Flat par fours can be dull and boring, but a good architect will try and liven them up in some way. He may put two bunkers in left and right at the front of the green. Beware of this, because it invariably has the effect he's looking for of foreshortening the hole.

If the yardage chart says 160 yards and you can't believe it's that far, then disbelieve the evidence of your own eyes.

The other person who can make a mockery of the yardage chart, of course, is Mother Nature. If the wind is howling, then 150 yards becomes a figure for negotiation, with obviously more club needed if you are playing into the wind and less if it is in your favour.

The wind can play immense tricks with a golf ball. The trick is to try not to hit it high so as to lessen its influence.

The professionals are great to watch in this instance. As I mentioned earlier in this book, keep your eye on a terrific wind player like Faldo. He won't be frightened of hitting a little knockdown five iron 130 yards if it means he can keep it under the wind and so control it.

This is the moment we step out on to the beautiful broad acres of the Oxfordshire Golf Club and pick six holes in which we can show you in practice some of the things we've been talking about in theory.

Ah, you ask: how can holes at the Oxfordshire be applicable to me when I never play them? Well, clearly we can't cover every situation, but most courses feature long and short par threes, fours and fives, and so we've picked one of each to demonstrate the sort of characteristics that you can expect to encounter.

FROM THEORY

Long par three
(5th hole, 205 yards)

There can't be anything that the average golfer finds more challenging than a death or glory short hole where he either carries the water or he doesn't. The first thing to observe here is playing it off its full length is daft unless you're a very good player.

Local professional Ian Mosey reckons it is a two iron for him off the back tees, so on this sort of hole you should be playing off the tees that would require you to use a four wood or three iron. The Oxfordshire has clearly thought of this: there are no less than seven tees from which to choose!

There's no really smart strategy you can use on a hole like this. You've got to approach it with a positive frame of mind and dismiss the water from your thoughts. Clearly it is a mightily tough challenge, but you're up to it, aren't you. Aren't you? Finally: swing smoothly. The smoother your swing is, the greater your chances of making the putting surface.

Short par three
(2nd hole, 141 yards)

Typically a short par three will feature a small green that is heavily bunkered. Think of the Postage Stamp at Royal Troon, so named because of the size of the green, or the fourth at Turnberry. Miss either green and you're looking at a five not a three. And why not? You've got a short iron in your hands, so if you miss the target you should be heavily punished.

This is a short par three with a difference. It has a large green, but there isn't a great deal of depth to it, so you have to be wary. Clearly the sensible shot here is to aim for the fat of the green. You'd kick yourself if you dropped a shot.

Because the hole is flat, this is one instance where you need to pay extra attention to its length. If you think it looks much shorter you will underclub, with disastrous consequences.

TO PRACTICE

Above: Try to dismiss the water from your thoughts when playing this shot. Imagine there is nothing but dry land between you and the pin, and swing smoothly.

Left: The green is very narrow where the pin is situated so aim for the left half, the 'fat' part of the putting surface.

1: A wonderful par four, where the more you aim towards the bunkers on the left, the shorter your approach shot.

2: Many players will find this a daunting prospect but don't be afraid to come up short and play for a bogey.

3: Seen from the back of the hole, one can see that all the trouble is at the front of the green. Clearly, if you have the length, the object would be to take one club more rather than force a shot.

Long par four
(9th hole, 405 yards)

This is a classic long par four. It is a dog-leg left and so the more to the left you drive your ball the less distance you will have to travel with your approach shot. But the corner of the dog-leg is protected by bunkers so you have to tread carefully here. Similarly, if you play too safe, you will not only be too far away to reach the green in two, but you will be blocked out by the rolling hills on the right of the picture.

The green has a narrow entrance but widens and has plenty of depth, and is therefore very forgiving, so a player can be bold here. The advantages of taking as much off the dog-leg as you dare are such that you need to be aggressive off the tee. If you have the ability to fade the ball, this type of hole is perfect for you. Be brave; don't be afraid to line up on the bunker and let the ball fade back into the fairway.

Whenever you approach this type of green, you should consider using one club more than normal, as all the trouble is at the front of the green. The very narrow entrance means that, if you can, you should take it out of play.

Of course, 405 yards may be outside your range in two anyway. Even if you can get up with your two Sunday-best shots, you should really play it as a par five. This is such a difficult par four that it is easy to score six in trying to obtain it. But it offers a straightforward chance to score five.

If you fit this bill you shouldn't be flirting with the bunkers on the left at all. Your approach should leave you about 70 yards from the green and a simple pitch and two putts at the worst.

Short par four
(6th hole, 320 yards)

Some of the best holes on any course are short par fours. Think of the 10th hole at the Belfry or the 12th at Sunningdale. In recent years there has been a trend to do away with the short par four because some macho golf course designers think there is no place for them, that the better players simply over-power them.

Thankfully the architect Rees Jones isn't a paid-up subscriber to this errant nonsense and he has come up with two beauties at the Oxfordshire. One is the 8th, where the player has to box clever around a lake, but the 6th is the sort of hole you might see on any good golf course, and so perhaps will serve our purposes better here.

The green is devilishly protected – they usually are on holes this length – and so the strategy here has to be to find the fairway with your tee shot. Ideally you want to leave yourself with a full nine iron or wedge shot, because that way you'll have more chance of stopping the ball.

The green is slightly elevated and so if you hit a nine iron 120 yards and you have 120 yards to play, you are really going to have to strike it well to get the distance. Short of the green is no place to be, so the smart play here should be a smooth eight iron, with your hands perhaps slightly further down the shaft than normal.

1: The idea here is not to end up in the bunkers that protect either side of the fairway so don't be afraid to play this hole with something like a five iron and then an eight iron.

2: The green is slightly elevated and so the second shot will play slightly longer than the yardage marked.

Left: Bunkers come in all shapes and sizes, for example at the Oxfordshire, where this book was photographed, the par five 4th hole features a bunker that is some 80 yards long.

Long par five (4th hole 545 yards)

This is a hole the like of which you may never have seen before! The middle of the fairway is dominated by a bunker that must be 80 yards in length from back to front, so clearly some added thought is needed. The members at the Oxfordshire must be decent fairway bunker players.

The hole is a dog-leg right and therefore the object of the exercise is to drive the ball long enough to leave you the opportunity of clearing the desert with your second shot.

One thing you mustn't do is be too greedy. A drive that finishes in the rough on the right, leaves a player looking at a six at best. Don't get intimidated by this type of hole. That's the effect the architect is trying to achieve. In fact if your drive finishes straight down the middle, clearing the sand ought not to prove such a problem with your second shot.

What if your ball goes to the left and now you know you can't clear the sand with your second? You have to be honest with yourself: how good am I out of fairway bunkers? If they hold no terrors, then blast away and take your chances. A fairway bunker will only cost you 20 yards at most and if you lay up short you're throwing away more than 80 yards and you have no chance of reaching the green in three. If you're absolutely terrible however (why are you after reading this book?) you may consider it a price worth paying.

The green is narrow to the left with plenty to aim at on the right. The pin is invariably on the left. If you've a wedge in your hands and you're confident with it, you may think it worth having a go at the pin, otherwise, make sure you hit the green. A par five on a long, long hole is never a bad score.

1: Don't try to be a hero on this sort of hole. Play for position number 2, rather than trying to carry the bunker on the right.

2: Quite why is obvious here. Finish in the bunker (3) and your dreams of a birdie have vanished, to be replaced by thoughts of a bogey or worse.

3: Playing for the fairway, however, allows you to carry the hazard with your second shot, setting up an approach to the green.

1: Intriguing options abound here. Should I go around the lake or across? The safer option is certainly 'B'.

2: The reason to go for 'B' is obvious here. For most high handicappers, this shot over water is a daunting prospect.

Short par five (17th hole, 490 yards)

Again, short par fives are invariably a focus for much excitement because of the possibility of scoring birdies and eagles. Augusta National has two classics with the 13th and the 15th, and the tournament is invariably won or lost on these two holes.

The 17th at the Oxfordshire is a perfect example of this type of hole. The penalties for someone who gambles and fails are severe, but the rewards for success are great.

In effect, there are two fairways, divided by an enormous water hazard. The boldest of drives allows you to cross the water for a relatively easy route for the rest of the hole. Indeed anyone who hits the ball a good length will be able to consider hitting the green in two shots. The other, safer option on the tee means the water is a factor for you for the rest of the hole.

Most players will have to go by this route. The glory offered by the first option is overwhelmed by the risk. Sure you could get a four. But you could also more easily be playing three from in front of the lake.

The trick on a hole like this is to try to dismiss the intimidating effects of the water from the mind. You've got plenty of room with your drive and also with your second shot, which will leave a straightforward pitch to the green. Why worry about the water?

The smartest ploy is to play the wood off the tee with which you feel most confident, to enable you to forget the lake on the left and hit the fairway. Now take a fairway wood or a long to medium iron – again the one with which you feel entirely comfortable – and pick out a spot where you want the ball to land and focus on it. The point about water holes is that once you've played them properly a couple of times, the fear element is then dramatically diminished. Thinking clearly is a big step in this direction.

3

3: Play sensibly around the water, however, and you can take it out of play, although you will be left with a much longer approach shot.

B

Glossary of golfing terms

A	Albatross	A score of three under par on a hole. In America it is referred to as a double-eagle.
B	Back-nine	The second set of nine holes on an 18 hole golf course. Sometimes referred to as the inward nine.
	Birdie	A score of one under par on a hole.
	Bogey	A score of one over par on a hole.
	Borrow	The amount a putt will deviate due to a slope of the green.
C	Carry	The distance from when a ball is struck to when it first lands.
	Chip	A low-running shot played from around the green to the putting surface.
D	Divot	A piece of turf removed when a shot is played.
	Dogleg	A hole that changes direction, either to the left or the right, halfway through its course.
E	Eagle	A score of two under par on a hole.
F	Fairway	The area of mown turf between tee and green.
	Fourball	A match between two teams of two players, each playing their own ball.
	Foursome	A match between two teams of two players, each playing one ball by alternate shots.
	Front nine	The opening nine holes on an 18 hole golf course. Sometimes referred to as the outward nine.
G	Green	An area of closely-mown grass prepared for putting.
H	Handicap	The system than enables players both to take on each other and the course on level terms. The worse a player is the higher the handicap and the more shots he receives. If someone regularly goes around a course in 20 over par then they should have a handicap of 20 and will receive 20 shots towards their efforts of matching the par of the course.

Hook	A mistimed shot that deviates severely to the left for the right handed player.
Lie	Situation in which a ball finishes after the playing of a stroke.
Long Iron	A description for those irons numbered 1-4
Matchplay	Form of the game where holes won and lost are the determining factor rather than strokes played.
Mid-iron	A description for those irons numbered 5-7
Par	The standard score for each hole, and the entire course.
Pitch	Lofted shot from around the green to the putting surface.
R&A	The game's governing body, the Royal and Ancient Golf Club of St Andrews.
Rough	The area of unmown grass that lies either side of the fairway.
Short iron	A description for those irons numbered 8-9, the pitching wedge, sand wedge, and indeed any other wedges.
Shank	Totally mistimed shot, usually with a short iron, where the ball comes off the junction between hosel and club-face and travels at right angles to the target intended.
Slice	Mistimed shot where the ball deviates sharply to the right for the right-handed player.
Strokeplay	Form of the game where the number of strokes played is the determining factor.
Sweet spot	The precise spot in the middle of the club where the greatest possible mass can be delivered from the club face to the ball.
Tee	Closely-mown area where the first stroke on a hole is played. The ball is generally played from a tee peg.
Yips	A nervous condition induced by poor chipping and putting which can render its victim totally unable to do either.

L

M

P

R

S

T

Y

INDEX

Numbers in italics refer to illustrations